Where Is My Father?

*A Young Man's Journey,
Towards A Positive Self Image.*

Bishop E. Edward Robinson, II

Go'Judah Publishing House

A Young Man's Journey Towards A Positive Self-image

E. Edward Robinson, II
New York, New York

Copyright © 2016 E. Edward Robinson, II. All rights reserved. No part of this publication may be reproduced, stored in or introduced into a retrieval system, or transmitted, in any form or by any means (electronic, mechanical, photocopying, recording or otherwise), without the prior written permission of the copyright owner.

The scanning, uploading, and distribution of this book via the Internet or via any other means without the permission of the publisher is illegal and punishable by law. Please purchase only authorized electronic editions and do not participate in or encourage electronic piracy of copyright materials. Your support of the author's rights is appreciated.

Unless otherwise stated, scriptures are quoted from the King James Version www.biblehub.com

Editors: Candice Briggs, Betsy Rosario
Formatting and Layout: Go'Judah Publishing House
www.gojudah.com 631.780.6877
Book Cover: Steve Asfall

ISBN 13: 978-0-9981777-1-7   ISBN 10: 0-9981777-1-7 **(paperback)**
ISBN 13: 978-0-9981777-0-0   ISBN 10: 0-9981777-0-0 **(hardback)**
ISBN 13: 978-0-9981777-2-4   ISBN 10: 0-9981777-2-4 **(e-pub)**

Where Is My Father?

<u>I Dedicate This Book…</u>

To Ebony, my beautiful wife and my three wonderful kids; Earnest, Nakiyah, and Nadiyah- Thank you for giving me the greatest privilege and honor, that is being a father.

To my awesome mom, Mother Audrey L. Robinson, who raised me in the fear of the Lord.

To my loving Father, Elder Earnest Robinson, Sr.

To my Apostolic Father, Bishop Arthur Linder, Sr.

<u>To all my Spiritual Fathers:</u>

Superintendent Robert Madison, under whom I received Christ.

Bishop Harrison Hale, under whom I grew up.

Bishop T.C. Cox, my Episcopal mentor.

To my good friend Ronald Crowe, Sr., I learned so much from you about business. Thank you for believing in me.

To my local church family, thank you for your prayers and support during this journey.

To my Fellowship of Covenant Churches, especially my 1st Vice Regent Overseer Willie Elliott, whom I affectionately call Dad Elliott, thank you for standing by my side.

I love you all. I am grateful for your time and dedication to my matriculation and development. You will never be forgotten for your invaluable contribution to my life!

ACKNOWLEDGEMENTS

I want to thank my covenant brother who really pushed me on this project, when I say pushed me, I mean pushed me! Pastor Lewis Dudley II you are the best!

At the last minute you were thrown in the water- and you swam! Thank you Betsy Rosario!

I also want to acknowledge my awesome "Ministry Opts" team, who worked tirelessly by my side assisting me to complete this project, you rock!

"To know the true state of a nation, look at the state of the Church. To know the true state of the Church, look at the families who populate our pews. To know the state of our families, look to the fathers who lead them. Destroy the vision of the father, and you render impotent the family, thus creating a chain reaction that spreads throughout civilization."

Douglas W. Phillips, Esq.

A Young Man's Journey Towards A Positive Self-image

THE FORWARD

How do we learn to appreciate truth when it's expressed clearly? I find Mr. Robinson did not hide behind the garments of his priestly anointing. In this book, he revisits places and events that are spoken of or describe at all, very little. He found the grace of God within to be very explicit. Applause is an understatement. if we were to conduct a research of the percentage of men and women who have suffered at the hands of a loved one and close friend, it will be immeasurable.

This is a manuscript that must be delved into with care and an open mind. **"Where is my Father" is not to hurt men, who have lost interest in the family structure, but to heal and empower man who never found themselves.** No one took a moment to walk them by the hand. Can the question be answered in this discourse? I believe it did. Have you carefully taken the time to see and study the pattern that exists among young fathers? Let us remove ourselves from criticism and stretch a helping hand to the men that we know that are in danger and despair, frustrated, angry and lost, let us bring HOPE to their lives and cause them to live again with a great pursuit for life.

+Christopher T. Cox, II.

A Young Man's Journey Towards A Positive Self-image

TABLE OF CONTENTS

Preface..11

CHAPTER ONE
My Genesis – The Call that Changed My Life......................16

CHAPTER TWO
What's the Difference?..27

CHAPTER THREE
The Father of the Bible – Rev. Daddy...............................41

Pages of My Life- Earnest has to die! He has a P-R-O-B-L-E-M...58

CHAPTER FOUR
The Speaker of the House..64

CHAPTER FIVE
Daddy's Girl..77

The Pages of My Life- I Found a Way to Kill Earnest............86

CHAPTER SIX
My First Hero Called Dad!..94

CHAPTER SEVEN
Grandfathers..102

CHAPTER EIGHT
The Sacrifices of The Father..111

The Pages of My Life – My New World and Old World,
*   Don't Want to Play Nice..................116*

CHAPTER NINE
Blessings of My Father...120

CHAPTER TEN
Stepping Back into Place (Part I)...132
    (Re-establishing a Relationship with Your Father)

CHAPTER ELEVEN
Stepping Back into Place (Part II)...145
    (Re-establishing a Relationship with Your Son)

The Pages of My Life – Mister President............................156

CHAPTER TWELVE
Father Figures .. *(with a Concentration on Spiritual Fathers)*.......163

CHAPTER THIRTEEN
Spiritual Sons... 182

CHAPTER FOURTEEN
Don't Be a Bastard..195

CHAPTER FIFTEEN
Our Father Which Art in Heaven.. 215

The Pages of My Life – Earnest Must Live:
    "I Shall Live and Not Die"............229

APPENDIX:
RESOURCES...247

A Young Man's Journey Towards A Positive Self-image

Preface

Why am I writing this book? Is it from a bitter space? Is it a tell-all? Does it come from a rebellious disposition? Will it incite sedition? Is it a rebuke to fathers? Or is it a rebuke to the sons? What is my motivation and agenda for this writ? These are the questions that may circle one's mind when they're first introduced to this title.

I want to put your mind at ease by telling you it's none of the above. This story is a young man's journey towards a positive self-image. It's my story. And many of you will learn it's your story as well. You may wonder, what is the connection between my father and my positive self-image? Well, hence the purpose of this book.

Statistical data regarding the positive and negative influence of an active father in the lives of his children or the lack thereof is staggering. From how well they do in school, their rate of success in life and their job, to relationships, they all are affected by fathers. Furthermore, (see appendix) research can prove that many of our youngsters in jail come from fatherless homes. Many suicidal cases are from fatherless homes. Many teenage or unwed pregnancies come from fatherless homes. Even many poverty cases are the direct effects of fatherlessness. On the flip side, an extreme amount of successful cases stems from having a present father in the household. I believe fathers are the key to building a better community and a productive and positive culture.

I believe this book will be a blessing to sons, fathers, spiritual leaders, wives, mothers and daughters. For it contains keen insight on who you are and/or dealing with in your life. For instance, if you are a wife, your husband is a son to his father whether the father is alive or not and whether they had a good or bad relationship. What is certain is that their relationship has helped to shape and play a very vital role in developing the man you see today. This book is a must read from every spectrum of the family and will give everyone a better grasp on how to help heal and/or release the power of fatherhood in their respective relationships.

For those of you like me, who grew up predominantly without a father, this book will help you discover things about yourself you never thought were there. It will also help bring closure to some unanswered questions, unresolved issues, as well as, a new exciting beginning for you and everyone your life touches.

For new or prospective fathers, this will serve to help equip you in your most glorious role to come. You will see for yourself how important you are to the family unit, according to God and society at large. You will realize how you play a huge part in shaping culture and systems of thought. Fatherhood, in my opinion, is the greatest weapon against darkness or light, good or bad, righteousness or wickedness. It all starts with the father!

As a spiritual leader, a Presiding Prelate of a Covenant Fellowship of Churches, a Senior Pastor of a local assembly as well as being an owner and executive director of a child daycare program, I realize more and more how the connection between real success and failure is centered on fatherhood. For those of you who are pastors and leading God's people, this book will serve as a reminder of how important your role as a spiritual father is to the sons and daughters of the Kingdom of God.

This information will open the eyes and hopefully the heart of every spiritual son to see from a son's perspective the necessity of identifying, embracing and submitting to your spiritual father. You will also see spiritual fathers from a different vantage point and grow to appreciate their value even more in the Kingdom of God.

Lastly, for the Christian believer, you will see the interplay and the overall connection that God has with the concept of fatherhood. You will see God in a new light and be inspired to foster a richer and more intimate relationship with this person we call God; the one who was once only perceived as The Lord of Hosts, the Almighty and All Powerful God but who will be made known to you today through this book as God The Father.

I know, by now, you are just itching to get to the meat of this book and be blessed by its contents. But just before you begin, I want to share with you that this book took over seven years to complete. Yes, SEVEN! Why? Well, it wasn't so much the actual writing that took so long, it was the process. As you read this book, you will also read my life's story. That was the part that took so long. The process of reconciling all my hurts, pains, anger, cover-ups and disillusions of success made this a very difficult project to undertake.

However, by the grace of God, I have the victory, and I want to share with you how I got it so that you might discover for yourself the role and power of a father in all our lives. Yes, in every area of our lives: physical, spiritual, and eternal. As you read, you will notice that my story begins in chapter 1 and is inserted throughout the rest of the book. They are called the "pages of my life." So let's get ready to go! Where? We are going to a place of healing, wholeness, clarity and ultimately towards a positive self-image.

A Young Man's Journey Towards A Positive Self-image

Chapter One:

My Genesis

The Call That Changed My Life

The phone call that changed my life forever came on a regular evening after school. The caller was my father and the subject is a most fitting commencement of this writing. Though my true genesis began seven years prior, of which we will deal with later. This phone call serves as the backdrop of the question posed in this book, **"Where Is My Father?"**

The Call

I can't remember the season. I can't remember the day of the week, but what I do remember is that it was in the afternoon and the initial honor of being chosen for such an awesome task. I thought I was ready. I remember the fireworks going off in my belly and the anxious anticipation of spreading the news that in retrospect, was one of the saddest tales to report.

The News

That afternoon my father called and though my memory is a little foggy on all the details, it was clear that I was charged with the responsibility of looking after my mom and family. I can remember he said the words, "You are the man of the house now. You have to look out for them for me." For a son, our greatest mission in life is to please and make our Father proud. So you can see why this was such an honor for me at the time. My father trusted me! He placed me in charge! I was now the "Man of the house".

The Problem

Unfortunately, I was still a little boy. I hadn't even gone through puberty yet. However, that didn't stop me from assuming the position. I took on this new role as a badge of honor! What came next was my big announcement to my siblings, "You have to call me Jr. Daddy." The crazy thing about this was that, I meant it. Even at such a young age, I knew my dad wasn't just the 'Man of the House', the 'Man' in charge, the boss, the big guy. He was our Father. So if I was the new man of the house I had to be my Father's representative. I didn't dare take his full place, so I settled for the title "Jr. Daddy". After all, my name was Jr. and his name was daddy.

Now if you have other siblings, you already know what came next. "Jr. you're crazy!" they yelled. But I wasn't. I wanted to make my father proud and show him that I was serious about the task he entrusted to me. Yet as serious as I was and as honorable as I found the mission, I was in no way ready for such a vast responsibility. As I alluded to earlier, I was just a little boy, only seven years old as a matter of fact. Yet I became the protector of my mother and guardian of my four siblings; two older and two younger. The funny thing was I had full confidence in my ability to fulfill such a daunting role because my father chose me. To me, he was the smartest, brightest, strongest man alive! So if he chose me, baby there was no doubt about it! I was the man, I mean boy! No let's just leave it at "The Man".

From that day on, I was transformed! I attempted to take charge. I was not about to let my family or my father down. I wanted to be ready to give him back the reigns of leadership upon his return with a good report from my mother, my brother, and my sisters. I had no idea that this was an indefinite position. There was no thought in my mind that he wouldn't be there for the rest of my childhood. For me, this was temporary. I didn't question where he was going because I was so sure he would return. Where and how long wasn't important to me because I expected him back at any moment. As you continue to read my story, you will find out what I had to discover, sadly he wasn't coming back, at least not in my youth. If I was able to grasp the reality of the situation I guess I would have pleaded, no, begged him not to go or better yet chose another father for the family because I wasn't able. Or maybe I would have even asked for more instructions to deal with the endless issues and problems that were sure to confront our family. I would have asked how to comfort mommy when she was lonely and how to discipline the kids when they became unruly. I would have asked how to interview prospective friends of my sisters to ensure that they would not be taken advantage of, how to pay the bills on time and when was a good time to have "the talk" with my young brother. It was all too fast and the call was too short. I could not think of all these things that fast. I was too selfishly proud of the fact of being chosen. I didn't think about how this would affect the whole family. All I could do was my best and attempt to make him proud!

Was my father going into battle and fearing his uncertain future? Did he get a bad doctor's report and have to put his house in order? Was he being taken away from us by the police or gangs like we had seen on TV? Nope, the story was classic. He and mom didn't work out and they could no longer live as husband and wife. The good news; he was still alive. The bad news; he was not there.

Please don't think this is going to be a pity party that I am throwing on paper or my attempt to dishonor my father. As I said previously in my introduction, this is a story of a young man's journey towards a positive self-image. You can't get to your result without starting at the beginning. I can't tell you my victories unless I share my struggles and battles. Only then can you appreciate my triumph and only then can God get glory out of my life's story.

<u>*Going way back:*</u>

Where Is My Father?

Before we go any further, let me take you back to my true beginning. I was born to Earnest Edward Robinson, Sr. and Audrey Lanett Robinson. A beautiful couple who both came from a strong Christian background. My mother was raised as a "PK" (preacher's kid). Both my grandma and grandpa were Gospel Preachers in New York from the borough of Brooklyn. My dad hails from Memphis Tennessee. He too was raised in a religious home with Sunday school teachers for parents and a host of bishops, pastors, prophets and all kinds of ministers in the family. I was the third of my parent's children and the first male child. All together there were five children; three girls and two boys. We weren't rich but didn't know we were poor. With such a great beginning, our family was thought to be successful.

Mommy was always home to send us off to school and greet us after school. Daddy was the hard working provider. The fun times were endless. Don't let me start on the crazy times my older sisters and I had creating and making up games to play. There was always laughter in the Robinson household. We would play slip and slide, pouring dish detergent and a little water on the hallway floor, then running and sliding from one end to the other. (Of course that was only after our parents went to sleep.) Another made up game was wall climbing where we would stretch out our arms and legs to the ends of the hallway or doorway and race to the top. In a Brooklyn project (special housing for the poor) the hallways and every other part of the building was our playground. With so much fun and laughter it was hard to believe that something was brewing underneath the surface. It appears the devil had it out for my family and was determined to make our lives a living hell!

At four years old, I could remember my babysitter forcing me to watch explicit sexual material and then acting it out with her. It was my first introduction to sexual activity and we didn't tell our parents. We were told if we did tell something bad was going to happen to us. Well, at four, it didn't take much to get the point across. Then my family went through some stormy weather, to say the least. One day, I was being disciplined by my mother and somehow something triggered. Due to her unbearable stress, she lost control of herself. By the time, she was finished, she was standing on top of me, beating me. Afterward, I was told to tell and show my teachers the scars on my back from the beating. At five years old I didn't know enough about reasoning or understand rhetorical speaking, so of course I did exactly as I was told to do. At that point, I was going to do anything I was told in fear of another beating. I went to school the next day and asked to show my teacher something. I remember three scenes:

1. Lifting up my shirt and bending over to show her my back.

2. Lifting up my shirt and bending over to show the school nurse my back.

3. Being home and lifting up my shirt and showing these strangers in my home my back.

After that, all I know is my dad was tearing up (which was a miracle because he never cried) mom was crying and then my brother, sisters and I were being taken away from my parents. Thank God, my Aunt and Uncle registered with what was then called **B. C. W.** (Bureau of Child Welfare) and was allowed to take us in while my parents satisfied the courts to win our return home (but at least, we were with family and all together). Even at five years old, it was clear to me that I was responsible for getting my mom and dad in trouble and worse, splitting up my family. What a load to carry for a little boy!

The devil wasn't through yet. He had just begun his big plans for me. While displaced from my home for my protection, something horrible happened that would play out on and on throughout my life until I learned how to deal with it and get healing. One of my older cousins sodomized me. This went beyond the works of our babysitter who would just make me play like I was doing something after forcing us to watch pornography. This was a grown man fully raping a five-year-old boy. Once again, I had to swear that I would not tell anyone or risk the pain of death. So I didn't! After all, it was me telling about my pain that got my family in this state to begin with and that was after my mom told me to tell. How many more issues would arise if I was told not to tell? The assault was so painful that I blacked out, my mind completely blocked it from my memory and I didn't even come to terms with the rape until I was about ten years old. I recovered this traumatic memory only after having nightmares of being raped. I began to piece it together until my mind made a full recovery of the things done to me on that fateful day.

Finally! We were back at home with my parents! What a reception! The whole house was redone: new living room set, new TV, new dinner table. I remember running to my room to see my new bedroom set. Life was grand! It was better than before, or so we thought. I remember taking long walks through the park with my daddy and him doing something with a dollar bill rolled up and held to his nose. I had no clue. As any kid would, I questioned: "Daddy, what's that?" "My medicine," he replied. The same answer was given when I saw him smoking, but with a little twist, "I am smoking this cigarette because I have a cold." "Ok daddy," I replied.

One late night, mommy wakes us up, we rush to put our clothes and coats on. I remember vividly getting on the elevator, the train and buses headed to my grandma's house. Something felt real funny. Somehow I knew things were wrong. In fact, I was right. Mommy was leaving daddy. She was not going to raise her children in a drug-infested home. After living with a few of her friends from church and family, she called a family meeting. She explained that she was in no position to run a household by herself and needed time to get herself together. She told us she had to place us in foster care for a little while so that she could quickly get herself established.

I could only imagine how difficult it was to do anything with five small children aged from 1 to 8 years old. She had to get a job, get an apartment, get furniture. So off we went for six months and once again our family was split up but this time across the five boroughs. Her visits were like moments in heaven and sunshine after a long winter night. Finally, that glorious day came. Six months felt like ten years, but mommy kept her word! She got a job, an apartment and furnished our three bedrooms, two bathrooms, large living room and dining room to receive all five of us. Together again! The Robinsons were reunited, but daddy wasn't there this time. Not too long afterward somehow daddy was back in the picture. I felt all was right watching the scene of him lying on the couch, on my mother's lap as she rubbed his head. For a brief moment, we were all reunited! Even Daddy was there!

Then the call came that would change my life forever! Daddy called to say; he wasn't coming back home and I was in charge. I had to be the man of the house. Feeling responsible for the first separation of my family, I believed that I created the snowball effect damaging our perfect family. This was my chance to fix it all. This was my chance to repair the damage, so that when daddy came back this last time he would not ever leave again. But over and over and over again, time and circumstance would cause me to ask the question again and again and again: "Where is my father?"

Chapter Two:
What's The Difference?

My experiences drove home the fact in my understanding of the family unit, one quickly comes to the realization that each role and part of "The Family" is vitally important! With that being said, I maintain that the Father is the centerpiece of the family. I believe that scripture supports my school of thought that everything comes from the father. Let's appreciate each of the four basic roles of a family unit: Father, Mother, Son, and Daughter (and also understand the difference with each compared to the father). It's not my agenda to put any role down and create a competition of importance with each one, but rather pull out the urgent vitality of the father in the family unit.

This is a good place to pause for clarity. When I speak of "family," I speak of the God ordained, established, and empowered family unit He created. It is my heart's desire that we return to the order established by our heavenly father and turn from the chaos that has been established by this world. Chaos in certain areas of our lives is inevitable and most necessary when we abandon the Order of God willfully, deliberately or subconsciously through culture and tradition or just perversion and simple disobedience to the laws of God. Anything out of order is broken. Anything broken is in pieces and therefore not whole. God desires us to be whole. He desires to heal our brokenness. He does that through Grace and Truth. For the truth shall set us free and grace empowers us to stay free. So, if our families are going to be healed, we must bring ourselves back to the order of God; for only through His order can our families be made whole.

Looking at God's ordained order for the family through His lens, let's preview each of the four basic components of the family. We start our screening with mothers. Even though our main focus is on fathers, I want to deal with the Mothers somewhat extensively. I think it's important that we appreciate her value to the family and have a good foundational understanding of her God-given placement within the family unit and some of our responsibilities to her as well.

Mothers are soft, warm, loving, caring and nurturing. King Solomon of the Ancient Israelites stated that a wise woman builds her house. What does this mean? Does she build the house literally? Does it imply that she's independent to the point that she needs no one, and, therefore, can build her house all by herself? Nay. "<u>Her Children</u> arise and call her blessed, her <u>husband also</u>, and he <u>praises her</u>" **Proverbs 31:28.**

King Solomon's statement says it all! It is sad that today we have stripped the Wife & Mother of her glory, calling her position in the family weak and subservient. But I beg to differ, for it is strong! It is mighty! The Wife and Mother's role is needed in the family. We need not just females who can carry offspring then spring off into a life unto themselves. We need women committed to the universal calling of wifehood. The Hebrew word for woman is wife. The word connotation of women is womb-ed-man. That is Man with a Womb, called Woman, which translates to the word wife. Therefore, both "wife" and "mother" are united in the one word: Woman -indivisibly connected to the God-ordained family model forever!

As aforementioned, the children rise and call her blessed. The Husband praises her! That's both a commendation and responsibility. The commendation to our mothers and wives must be the responsibility of her children and husband.

Another clarity we must make before I can continue is that "we" (the members of the family) all are called to submit and serve one another. Each of us contributes to the success of the family. I placed that here because some, especially in the western hemisphere (culture), have declared that the wife is a slave and the mother a "less than"; au contraire, service to her family is not rendered against her will or by force as slave; however, each individual family constructs their chore list and corporal responsibilities, they each submit their services in love and out of a free will offering to each other. Yet as I alluded to earlier, some feel the traditional role of homemaker and stay-at-home mom to be subservient and a major step back for the feminist movement. We must stand up and 'Call the Mother, Blessed and Praise the Wife!' If we don't, society will continue to tear her down! Therefore, consider the Apostle Paul's charge to the Romans in the twelfth chapter of his letter to them; "Be Not Conformed to this world, (translated culture), but be ye transformed by the renewing of your mind."

The admonishment from the Apostle is to reject what "modern" day culture teaches, when it's not in submission or alignment to the <u>order</u> and <u>Word of God</u>. Instead, we must beg the mother to take her place and the wife to keep her stand. For a home without a Wife and Mother is no home at all. She makes it home. She is the common denominator that connects the family together. Without her, the children are mere seeds bound in the father, who is only a father because those seeds were released to her and she presents those seeds back to him as children from her womb.

Likewise, with vision and dreams, the father casts his seeds and she produces realities of his dreams. Does this make her less than, because she's playing such an important role in his dreams? Nay. For What God has joined, let no man put asunder! This not only tells us to beware of trying to separate God ordained relationships, but it also speaks of its imperativeness. Why must we keep from attempting to destroy God ordained unions? Because only God ordained unions produces God ordained purposes! There is a higher calling to your union than just being physically attracted or having things in common or a good partnership. There are deep seeds of greatness inside both the husband/father and wife/mother. When it's a God match with both working together to fulfill their destinies, it just happens to fulfill their separate destinies collectively. The submission of the wife is not the death of her dreams and visions. It is the divine synchronization of them with His Will, His Plan, and His Timing along with unity of her husband. As you can see, you cannot have a Wife/Mother as defined by the Bible without a Husband/Father.

Now let's look at another key player in the family unit; the son. I strongly believe sons are for posterity of the bloodline. They are the seed carriers and name extenders. They not only extend through reproduction, but they extend by conquest. Using a kingdom mindset, they help to extend the territory of the family land. They are protectors of both the name and domain. As long as there is a son to a household, that household shall never be dead. For the son carries the father's name out of the past and extends it to the future, in a sense, making the father immortal. The sons are the fathers of the next generation. One of the greatest signs that God is pleased with a father is the gift of a son. God is saying I want your name to remain in the earth's domain. Sons are then a reward from God the Father. We will deal more about "son-ship" in the chapters to come. A family unit without a son is a name soon to be cut off the earth. For only sons carry the blood of the family line, giving spiritual, natural and physical legal right for the family name to live in the land of the living. **1 John 5:7-8** *"For there are three that testify: Spirit, the water and the blood; and the three are in agreement." (NIV)*

Now, does this mean that daughters are a curse? NOT AT ALL! For daughters become gifts from God. **Proverbs 19:14** *"House and riches [are] the inheritance of fathers: **and a prudent wife [is] from the LORD.**"* That word prudent has a few meanings from the biblical application. I want to highlight two: "To show oneself attentive, to look or to cause prosperity."

Let's establish that every good and perfect Gift comes from God the Father. Therefore, daughters who grow up to be women or rather I say mature to be women, become a part of the pool from which God selects as a gift to a man and his family. That's awesome!

The above Proverb is telling us that a Father can within his right give an inheritance to a son, a good one at that. While other translations of this text even say a self-sufficient household, meaning the land, and all the bells and whistles, all pays for itself. But only God can give that son a wife that will be so attentive that she causes him to prosper! Now, we must consider prosperity. Is it just money, or houses or land? Not at all! Prosperity deals with success and success is not just about the Benjamin's baby. It's about legacy. It's about destiny. It's about purpose! A wife from God ensures her husband's destiny and purpose is fulfilled not just for him but for the whole family. He might indeed carry the seed of greatness in the form of potential, but if she doesn't receive it and birth it, it will forever remain a seed. We would only see a glimpse of what could have been in the earth but never it's reality, certainly not it's Full manifestation.

I personally believe daughters are a secret weapon for unity. Families and households are united by marriages. Enemies have become family through the daughters' marriage. They have the power to join two worlds together and ensure peace. They also have the potential to cause war, but we won't go there in this book. Again daughters cannot exist without fathers. Fathers cannot come into being without being born of a mother who has received the seed of the husband/father.

Every man has the potential to be a father, for he carries seed. But without women, his potential as a father will never manifest. Likewise, without a man, she could never be a natural mother in the fact that she bore children. Now, is this to say that all sons are a gift from God and only daughters who grow into womanhood and become a wife are gifts from God? Absolutely not. There are sons who worked to destroy their family, father's life work and themselves. There are women who never marry or bear children but have been proven to be gifts of God to the world at large.

A great example of this is *Mother Teresa of Calcutta*. Though not a wife or mother in the biological sense, she was indeed God's gift to humanity. Her love for God and His children from all shapes, sizes, colors and backgrounds caused her to live an exemplary life of service, caring for the poor, the sick, and those who society forgets.

Let's go back to our subject at hand, the father, because it starts with him. Remember, he holds the seed until it is released to the woman. However, just exchanging seed does not in its entirety spell out parenthood. We must rise above just being a seed donor and an egg carrier and become gifts from God to the world as fathers and mothers. In this book, we will stretch out fatherhood. So now that we have a seed and that seed was given to the woman, the woman gave birth to a child. That child is here and they ask, **"Where is my father?"**

Can we find him in a mentor?

A mentor is a guide who can help the mentee to find the right direction and develop a plan for careers, goals or issues. Mentors rely upon having had similar experiences to gain an empathy with the mentee and an understanding of their plight.

In Greek mythology, Odysseus written by Homer, we see Penelope as the wife of Odysseus, who was the king of Ithaca, a hero and great warrior. They were the parents of one son Telemachus, who was born just before the father was called away to fight in the Trojan War. After waiting faithfully for twenty years for his return, Penelope longed for his return for herself and her son. Her good friend Athena wanted to help them, so she took the disguise of mentor [another old close friend] so she would not be recognized by Penelope's suitors. As Mentor, the goddess Athena who was the daughter of Zeus, was the goddess of wisdom; she used her wisdom to encourage Telemachus to stand up against his mother's suitors and to never give up hope and most importantly to continue to search for his father and bring him back home. As you can see, even in Greek mythology the role of the father was paramount. Even the wisdom of the mentor could not replace the role of the father.

Because of Mentor's relationship with Telemachus, encouragement (from the disguised Athena) and practical plans for dealing with personal dilemmas, the name <u>Mentor</u> has been adopted in English. The term mentor means someone who imparts wisdom to and shares knowledge with a less experienced colleague. What I find interesting here, is that the Mentor is encouraging the mentee to search for his father. What irony!

Every father must be a mentor, but not every mentor is a father. A mentor can help the mentee because now the mentor looks at the mentee and sees a past version of himself, and the mentee looks up to the mentor and sees a potential future view of himself. A father looks at a son and sees past himself to see his seed's destiny! (Not the father's, but the son's own destiny.) He's not trying to turn the son into him, but he pulls out what's inside to help shape a destiny that transcends a singular purpose or temporal activity, or even a mere material desire of things, but rather a Godly calling of predestined purpose. No mentor can do that! Only a father can see that far into a seed, to accomplish such a glorious outcome. For the seed to a father is at first a mirror of himself but then a window into the future becoming the picture of his legacy.

I suggest everyone seek out a mentor for every major goal in your life. Their wisdom is priceless. Experience is a treasure chest of knowledge fit for a king!

Notice, Mentor from our Greek story, encouraged her mentee to search out his father. She understood that a mentor teaches, guides and instructs <u>but on a deeper level a father deposits, imparts and activates.</u> A mentor can inform you, but a father is the only legal agent in the realm of spirit and nature that can reproduce and yield a legitimate heir. <u>A mentor gives you what they know, but a father pulls out of you what he imparted into you when he released the seed that made you.</u> This is the developmental process that once completed can only be activated by the father's blessing.

<u>Can I find the same value of fathers in FRIENDS & brothers?</u>

"A friend loves at all times and
a brother is born for adversity."
Proverbs 17:17,

A true friend's bond is somewhat eternal in that it doesn't end. Friends accept you for you. I would go as far as to say, friends not only accept who you are but they celebrate you. Not only do they celebrate you for who you are, but they are one of the first to congratulate you on where you are in retrospect to where you were and where you're going.

"Brothers are born for adversity". We are tempted to interpret that as an explanation for the many fights we may have had with our brothers growing up. But I don't think this is what the writer means. Brothers will fight for each other, not just with each other. Brothers are connected on a greater level than friends, because we elected to bond with certain friends; nevertheless, brothers are God's choice.

Friends love until the end by choice. Brothers fight for each other through a blood connection, but even so, they are not on the same level compared to fathers. A brother cannot instruct, impart or even bless in the same natural and spiritual authority of a father. A friend knows they can encourage and admonish, but no one wants a friend trying to act like a father. So they come up short in the vital role a father must play in the life of his children. Siblings and friends cannot compare or substitute. There is a blessing that can only come from the father! No other party in the family can bestow a father's blessing but a father.

As we close this chapter, I believe you can now see the importance of and appreciate each role in the traditional family unit as well as the vital role that our mentors and friends play in our lives. Moreover, above all roles, we are establishing the necessity and key imperative of having the father's presence amongst them all.

Chapter Three:
The Father of the Bible

"Rev. Daddy"

What is a father and what are his responsibilities per the teachings of the Bible? Allow me to pull a quote from the Jewish scribe of *Shemot Rabbah* (Exodus Rabbah)

"He who brings up a child is to be called its father, not he who gave birth."

Wow! What a statement, from this we can clearly see that the responsibilities of the father are much greater than just reproducing. The scripture says to raise up a child in the way he should go. To raise up is the operative phrase. Therefore, it is not what we put in a woman (seed) that makes us a father. That merely proves that we are seed bearing males. However, what we put in our seed is what makes us fathers!

According to my research of the ancient Hebrews, the father is obligated to circumcise, redeem (*pay a tribute to God in place of giving him to God, especially the first-born sons, they belonged to God by divine right*), to teach the Torah, acquire a wife for and teach a craft to the sons. The word father appears in the Old Testament (The Hebrew Bible) 1212 times. The number [12] in the Bible represents perfect governmental foundation. Just looking at this number "12-12" provides us with a clue as to the important relationship the father has in helping to shape the foundation for a perfect government. To put it another way, producing a prosperous society all begins with fatherhood. The base of the word father is the first letter of the Hebrew alphabet. The Hebrew word for father is AB, which means chief. The Greek word for father is patér – father; one who <u>imparts life</u> and is <u>committed to it</u>; a progenitor, bringing into being to pass on the potential for likeness.

It occurs 418 times in the New Testament. To occur over 1600 times, not including its many other variations, it's obviously a big deal.

Genesis 2:24 *Therefore, shall a man <u>leave</u> (loosen) his father and his mother, and shall cleave* (pursue and cling) *unto his wife: and they shall be one flesh."* Here we find the word Father first introduced to us in the Holy Scriptures, right after the formation of the woman and her presentation to Adam. The principle here in the word leave implies a sense of severing from one to be joined and connected to another. Is it possible that we can pull some insight on the role of the father, out of this verse that is normally the foundational text for marriages? I think so.

Working with the definitions from the vantage point of fatherhood, as afore stated, this is the first time we see the word "father" presented to us in the Bible. Second, we see a commandatory tone of voice used to express the thought. What's key is the "therefore". The text starts with, therefore, suggesting that this statement is made on account of another. In order words, what is being said now is based on previous statements prior, which are found in *Genesis 2:18-20.* I encourage you to take a pause and read this scripture before you go any further in this chapter.

Before we can deal with the clause of the "therefore", we must first deal with the prior statement which is: **Genesis 2:18** *"<u>And the LORD God said it is not good that the man should be alone;</u> I will make him a help meet for him."*

1. God declares it's not good for man to be <u>alone</u>. That word <u>alone</u>, is [bad]ad in Hebrew, and it means to be separated by himself. (Badad comes from the base word bad which means empty.) Our English word for <u>alone</u> originates from Middle English, from *al* (*all + one*). *Meaning:* without help from anyone or anything else, without another, without including or needing anything more. without aid or support.

   So in short, God declared it is not good for man to be "Badad" (*separated by himself*), or rather that it is "bad" (*empty*) for a man to be "ALL + One" (*without any aid or support*).

2. Also, note that this is the first time in the account of creation that God uses the term "not Good' in describing his creation. Read Genesis, chapter one. Look for everything God created and notice how HE saw it, and then declared it Good. Now look at this **Gen 1:31** "And God <u>saw everything that</u> he had made, and, behold, <u>it was very good.</u>"

3. God not only observes, but HE moves to correct the problem. He pulls a rib out of Adam, making

him incomplete. Now he is found wanting. Now he is in need. God forms from his rib, a woman. He makes and shapes her then presents her to Adam. God steps back and waits to see what Adam should call her. He decides to call her woman! He calls her wife! He identified that she is the right one for him! Out of all the creatures in the earth, she is the only one for him! Together they become one, The One that God intended. Finally, Adam like the rest of creation, has his, "Good Thing". As the scripture says, *"when a man finds a wife, he finds a good thing"*.

4. Now man reflects the image that was in the Mind of God when He said *"Let us make mankind in our image, after our likeness." So God created mankind in His image, in the image of God He created them; male and female he created them. God blessed them and said to them, "Be fruitful and increase in number,"* **Gen 1:26-28**.

Seeing that we now have a greater understanding of what came before to establish the "therefore". That is, from dirt, man was formed, and thus from man the woman was formed. Once God has formed the women, He will present her to the man (the husband) as the right, suitable-helper, aid-support to the man called of God, walking in divine destiny.

Just note, that the man and woman start out at home in their respective father's house as sons and daughters developing, being processed and matriculated. So that by the time God presents the formed and made woman to the mature man, he's ready to be the man of the house. Then, they (husband & wife) both transition from being fathered and mothered to becoming a father and mother.

From the time of divine presentation, he should leave, in the form of loosening himself from his father and mother and cleave (fasten) himself to his Wife! So much so that they go from two to one, in that process they become one flesh, one man, as God saw from the beginning of creation.

How does this relate to fatherhood? Look at it! **All of Adam's family was literally inside of him.** His wife and children were inside of him as the father. **He was the source from which his family was pulled out of.** So, as we begin our journey on the discovery of the biblical father, we start here in the beginning, with the initial presentation of the family as orchestrated and directed by God, the Heavenly and Ultimate Father.

Remember, the word for father is also the first letter of the Hebrew alphabet. It denotes that the father is not just the chief or head because of his male gender, but rather because he's first on the scene and all of the family comes out of him. It's also because he's the covering for the family, just as the first letter covers the alphabet, so the father covers his family.

Let's flow through different fathers of the Bible to see what we can learn from them. We already dealt with Adam from the perspective of the source of which the entire family is pulled from. Now let's look at Job.

There was a man in the land of Uz, whose name was Job; and that man was perfect and upright, and one that feared God, and eschewed evil. And there were born unto him seven sons and three daughters. His substance also was seven thousand sheep, and three thousand camels, and five hundred yoke of oxen, and five hundred she asses, and a very great household; so that this man was the greatest of all the men of the east. And his sons went and feasted in their houses, every one his day; and sent and called for their three sisters to eat and to drink with them. And it was so, when the days of their feasting were gone about, that Job sent and sanctified them, and rose up early in the morning, and offered burnt offerings according to the number of them

all: for Job said, It may be that my sons have sinned, and cursed God in their hearts. Thus did Job continually.

Job 1:1-5

Of course, we can pull from this that, Job was a great example to his children as a provider and sustainer. The Bible says "A good man leaves an inheritance for his children's children". Job was definitely a good man. He amassed so much wealth that he was considered the greatest man of his people or the richest man of that region. Job was a man of integrity and of good character as well. Wealth and good character are not normally married, but He was indeed a Godly man. Now here's what I loved the most about him, <u>he led his family by example to worship, even to the point where he worshiped on their behalf.</u>

Job severed as priest of his house, offering up sacrifices unto God (an act of worship) on their behalf. Today we see most men sending their wives and children to church while they stay home to rest and watch the game or go fishing or golfing. But Job beat his entire family to church and worshipped the Lord for his whole family! Wow!

Now, really, this is my favorite part:

But now stretch out your hand and <u>strike everything he has,</u> and he will surely curse you to your face."

His wife said to him, "Are you still maintaining your integrity? Curse God and die!"

He replied, "You are talking like a foolish woman. Shall we accept good from God, and not trouble?"

In all this, Job did not sin in what he said.

Job 1:11; 2:9; 2:10

Yes, it's kind of easy to bless God from the mountain top, but the question is; Can you be an example of faithfulness in the valley? Job was in the valley of his life with no promise of coming out. Matter of fact, it is believed that Job is the oldest book of the bible. If that is true, then that would mean that there were no written historical references for Job to go on, to guide him through his storms. So, he would really have to trust God at a point in his life where he could not trace Him or even have a hope of change in his condition. Yet, *"Job did not sin in what he said"*.

Above all for me Job was a perfect example to his entire family and even to us the world, on how to go through our seasons of test and trials. That legacy is far greater than the earthly wealth and prestige. His character remained intact or as his wife said "he maintained his integrity". That's a man, one who maintains his integrity in the midst of great adversity.

Job was an integral worshipper! God was God period! Job was going to worship God, period! And that was that, period!

What can we pull from Job's example on fathering? Though we face many challenges in life, we have to remember that as the fathers we are the leaders of our family. We must lead them in the right path. We must maintain a heart of worship and good character whether in good health or bad, a great house or poor, God's favor or His hand of testing.

Abraham

Then the word of the LORD came to him: *"This man will not be your heir, but a son who is your own flesh and blood will be your heir."* **Gen 15:4**

If you take the time to read the entire narrative of Abraham's transition from childlessness to the Father of Faith and multitudes, as accounted in *Genesis chapters 12 through 19*, you will come to realize that Abraham wanted to be a father! He was not running away from it! He valued the privilege of being a dad. He wanted to leave all that he accumulated his entire life, to a son, his son but was concerned that it might be left to a servant Eliezer. But I digress.

Eliezer must have been some kind of servant to be named as the only possible alternative for a natural born son. He must have been faithful and trustworthy. But in all of that, he would not inherit Abraham's estate, not because he wasn't worthy, but because God had bigger plans for Abraham, than just leaving it to one man. God set it up that Abraham will bless everyone. We all will get an inheritance from him. Abraham's seed will be blessed and a blessing to all mankind.

It is also important to note that Abraham was called into covenant with God. God changes his name from Abram (exalted father) to Abraham (exalted father of multitudes). This verse is Key:

<u>On that very day</u> Abraham took his son Ishmael and all those born in his household or bought with his money, every male in his household, and circumcised them, as God told him. Genesis 17:23

Abraham didn't procrastinate; he moved at God's word! What a good example to his son, his family and everyone that was under the covering of his household. He moved his family into right alignment with God! Into covenant agreement with God! Everybody in his household was lead into covenant relationship with God. What an awesome view of a Father! Here we see one of the most important roles of a father; **and that is to bring and lead his entire family into a personal relationship with God; into the perfect will of God for their lives.** He can only do that when he undergoes this same process himself. "Abram" had to go through a spiritual metamorphosis and be completely transformed, therefore being called "*Abraham*".

He went from just being an "exalted father" to an "exalted father of multitudes". My fellow fathers, we can't just settle on being called daddy or being lifted up in pride because we are the man of the house, the one in charge, the "exalted father". Instead it is important to allow God through the Holy Spirit to change us and bring us to the place where we are the "*exalted father of multitudes*"; effecting true change in our generation and leaving a legacy of change for the generations behind us. Pastors, we can't just be ok with being called a pastor to just our nice congregations, we must cause generational shifting, we must affect change that will linger in the earth realm and resemble heaven's will.

It will first take changing ourselves, our system of beliefs and mindsets; bringing personal and private thought into conformity to the will of God! Then and only then can we really lead our families into such covenant relationship with God. From Job, we see a father worshiping for his son and daughters. But from Abraham, God requires this father to lead his family into worship. There is a fundamental difference, from me going to church and praying for my family and me bringing my family to church and leading them into the prayer. What a glorious day, when the sons of God will lead their family to church and not send them to church with a prayer request at best!

Jacob

Let's look at Jacob and see what we can pull from him.

Abraham's grandson, Jacob had to undergo this same process that he went through. Jacob had to come out of his father (in-laws house), gather his family and bring them all into right relationship and covenant with GOD. But Jacob had some unfinished business to resolve: See he tricked Esau his brother into selling his birthright to him for a pot of porridge. Esau vowed to kill him, so Jacob has been on the run now for over twenty years. Before GOD could bring him to the next level of covenant relationship, Jacob had to resolve this family issue. GOD leads Jacob to the path of Esau. Therefore, in order for Jacob to go further into his destiny he must face his family issues.

It was there that Jacob goes up the mountain and meets GOD! It was there that we learned that Jacob wrestles with GOD, and his name is changed to *Israel*. In Hebrew, the meaning of the name Israel is: *May GOD prevail. He struggles with GOD. GOD perseveres; contends.* To be clear, Jacob wasn't fighting God as much as he and God teamed up to battle his old man for his destiny. They won! He went up Jacob and came down Israel. GOD changes his character, his core values even to the point that his walk was different, literally! Therefore, it's only befitting that GOD changes his name!

Let me go into a little church talk, we don't need a new title, we need a new name. Titles can sometimes make us think we are something we are not. Titles come before our name, almost shielding us from the realities of our mess. However, when GOD changes our name, we don't need a title to make us look good, as He said to Abraham, "I will make your name great!" As you change, your name will be changed to match the new you! HE did the same thing for Jacob and can do the same for you!

Armed with his new mindset, new heart and realigned spirit, Jacob is ready to face his brother and correct the issue and bring reconciliation to his family. Oh did you think that GOD will allow him to skip this part because he had a mountain experience? Absolutely not!

Sometimes we are disillusioned and think that because we have a mountain experience we don't have to face our issues. But I say it is the mountain experience that gives you the strength, wisdom, and understanding on how to face your problems. So just like Israel, we must seek reconciliation with our family. This was important to me because for years I thought I could not allow my family to distract me from reaching my GOD given destiny, <u>GOD had to reveal to me that I would never reach my destiny without my family.</u> (Those whom HE charged me to cover, protect and lead). It's almost like GOD said you can come to the finish line. But if you are here by yourself because you left, abandoned or forsook your family, you have to go all the way back and find where you left them and then come back to the finish line with them. **<u>You do not win by yourself.</u>**

GOD pretty much says to Jacob, this is as far as you're going, before I require you to face your past, to get to your future. **Men, you can't just move on; you**

must move right. Sometimes we can be stubborn and say I don't need them, but the truth is we do. We must fight our pride, hurt, or whatever may stop us, so we can bring ourselves into the perfect will of GOD, now we can face our family and make things right. Then we can move on with no bounty over our heads. Moving not as fugitives but as free men.

This applies to those who may have broken families. **You may have broken a romantic relationship with the mother of your children, but that broken relationship does not break your responsibilities as a father to your children.** You can't just start over with a new woman and forget about the kids you had with the other. It's not fair to them; it's not Godly. You have to go to the mountain of GOD so you can have the strength to reconcile with your family and bring them too, into covenant relationship with GOD!

Remember, GOD wants to make our name great not merely our title in church, nor just our position in life great. Our family bears our name; our sons carry on our name, so all of this is connected to the promise of greatness. Never forget it or neglect it. Also, <u>**keep note that the nation will come out of us! Sometimes we take it as something to conquer, no; this is something to give birth to.**</u> Therefore, we need our wives and sons and daughters if we are ever going to become the exalted father of multitudes.

As I conclude this chapter, by now you should see from our four examples *(Adam, Job, Abraham and Jacob)* that before there was centralized, systematic worship set up, with temples, formal priest and pastors; there was a Father. A Daddy who served as the priest of his household, the Pastor of his family. We shall call him Rev. Daddy.

Let's break here and return to my journey towards a *positive self-image.* then we will get back to our main subject line.

A Young Man's Journey Towards A Positive Self-image

The Pages of My Life:

Earnest has to die! He has a P-R-O-B-L-E-M!!!

Sad to say, it seems as though I was a target for sexual abuse. Throughout the course of my life I continued to be molested and forced into sexual activity. It was as though I showed up on the predator's radar appearing ripe for picking. For years I blamed my father for not being there to protect me, to defend me or to avenge me. It was these horrible acts which fed my thinking that there was something in me attracting such cruelty. A great inner hate began for me A poor self-image was being born.

I began to hate everything about myself; the way I walked, talked, laughed, played, dressed, even the way I ate. I could not stand the fact that there was something in me attracting men. There had to be something grossly wrong with me. I had to carry a signal, a sign or a banner that said, "here I am, come and get me. For me it wasn't just the men who abused me that hurt my self-image, it was the fact that kids my age would shout out to me, "You're a faggot!" "You're gay!" Don't get me wrong; everybody has a free will. They have a right to be and do what they want. But what was most hurtful, being that way wasn't what I wanted for myself. I did not want to be a faggot, I did not want to be gay! I did not desire to be in a sexual relationship with a man. However, because of everything that was going on, I hated myself! I started to believe that maybe they were right; maybe I am what they say I am. Maybe that's why he raped me and molested me. There's something in me that calls to them. For that, I hated me! I hated whatever I thought they (the predators) saw in me.

I knew that homosexuality was against God's will for humanity. I knew what the church taught, preached and what God's word said about it. What made matters worse is that I thought God didn't love me because of it. Even at a young age, I was very spiritual. I accepted Jesus in my life at the age of seven. So I knew God's will for my life was better

A Young Man's Journey Towards A Positive Self-image

than that. What did a lot of damage was thinking that God hated me because of what someone had done to me. For me, it was one thing for God to be displeased with me because of my disobedience to His word and or will. However, to force me into a hated situation with God and it is not my fault, that was crazy! That was unfair! How could God hate me for what he should have protected me from! Then I began to think that God let me down! He was supposed to cover me!

He was supposed to protect me! I never doubted God being real; it was a question of my being worth his time and attention. I felt I was not deserving of His saving grace or hand of protection. That's a lot for a man or a boy to handle. With all the moves and the abuse, of course, my behavior was affected at school and home. Needless to say, I was always in trouble. I can still hear my babysitters telling my mother and older siblings, "Jr., has a P-R-O-B-L-E-M! Yup, that's how she said it. She didn't say the word. She would spell it out. I had a problem! Their words confirmed it was me! I carried that with me for most of my life. I was the P-R-O-B-L-E-M at home, school, everywhere! I was the issue.

In school, it was because of my inability to control my emotions. I was always losing it, always crying, throwing temper tantrums and just acting out. I was put in special education and would continue there until I graduated high school. Needless to say, I never went to anyone of my high school reunions. For us, special education meant "off" or different. They were "sick in the head", slow and drooled... they were special. Guess what? I was one of them! The torment of just being in those classes was like being in a crazy house when you're not crazy. Great! My new nickname was, "special Ed faggot". That was just wonderful!

The self-hate grew and grew and grew and grew! I was a nobody. Now when I was growing up, being gay was nothing to celebrate, especially being black. Black men were supposed to be hard! Big dogs! Sexually driven! Manly! I was emotional and

A Young Man's Journey Towards A Positive Self-image

I was soft. According to them, I was gay! Even society was not open to the idea of being gay. Back then it was taboo; a celebrity's career was over when "they came out of the closet".

I'm not a gay basher. I am a holiness preacher. It is my belief that according to the word of God, His will is for man and woman, husband and wife. Again, I knew that. Guess what? I was not gay, but everybody called me gay. They treated me like I was gay!

This only grew the hate for myself, an even greater hate for my father and a huge disappointment towards God. I hated my father because I believed that had he been there, he would not only protect me from my predators and abusers, but he would model what a man was supposed to be. I realized that all the people in my house were women except for my little brother! I could not copy my little brother because then I would be acting like a baby. So without realizing it, subconsciously I would mimic what I saw from my big sisters and my mother. If dad was there I could model after him. If he saw something off with me that did not fit into the mold of being a man, (I mean a real man) he would stop it! Yes, he would!

So I had a P-R-O-B-L-E-M. I had to do something about my P-R-O-B-L-E-M! I had to kill myself! Yes! Earnest had to die! Earnest was left by his father. Earnest was molested. Earnest was raped by both men and women. Earnest was physically abused. Earnest was always ruining things for the family. Earnest was even hated by God, who literally was Love! How could you make love hate you? Ask Earnest! Earnest was a special Ed faggot. So again, Earnest had to die!

Chapter Four:

<u>The Speaker of the House</u>

As we refocus our attention to the father. In this chapter my goal is to discover *what is a father really, and what is his role as it pertains to the identity and self-image of his children.*

"After being baptized, Jesus came up immediately from the water; and behold, the heavens were opened, and he saw the Spirit of God descending as a dove and lighting on Him and behold, a voice out of the heavens said, This is My Beloved Son, in whom I am well-pleased."   **Mathew 3:16-17**

Now that we have established the importance of a father and some of his functions in the family unit, let's go deeper and attempt to approach this from a psychological perspective pulling on the example set before us by God the Father, in his relationship with Jesus the Son. We see a few things happening. The most important thing happening here is the Father Pro[**claim**]ing Jesus as His son! He is giving public notice that "this boy right here, is my boy." Isn't that an awesome feeling to be claimed by our fathers instead of being disowned, rejected and neglected by them? The Father decrees *"this is my son"*. What does that do for Jesus? It sets him apart. It charts his course in life and affects how he sees himself.

Yes, our daddy is our first mirror. It is through the father that we gain our self-image. The father plants the seeds of our self-image whether positive or negative. **Great fathers cultivate that seed and allow it to grow into full maturity.**

In *Luke (3:38)*, the Gospel writer establishes God as The Father of Man, specifically Adam, when he wrote *"the son of Enoch, the son of Seth, the son of Adam, the son of God."* This was Luke's genealogical presentation of Christ connecting his blood line all the way to Adam. We already pointed out that Adam embodied all humanity, therefore, if Adam was the son of God, God fathered not only Adam but mankind that proceeded from him.

Just before we deal with God 'THE' Father relationship with Jesus 'THE' Son, I want to focus on God 'THE' Creator (Father) and Man, the Created son.
God made man in His image. Therefore, the seed of self-image does indeed come from the father, God being the first father setting the example for all fathers. God's thumbprint is undeniably stamped on mankind and establishes Adam as HIS earthly first born. We emphasize Adam as HIS "earthly" first born son, because Jesus is God's only begotten Son, who was brought forth before the foundations of the world.

And GOD said, Let US make man in our image, after our likeness: and let them have dominion over the fish of the sea, and over the fowl of the air, and over the cattle, and over all the earth, and over every creeping thing that creepeth upon the earth. **Genesis 1:26**

From Genesis, we see that God first speaks and says, "*let US make the man.*" Then HE begins to identify what this man should look, act and be like. Now as natural fathers we don't have such great power to determine every detail of our children. **However, we can play a great role in shaping their self-image and how they perceive themselves which will affect how the world around them sees them.**

What we can learn from God's example as the first father is, the power of our words! Remember God 'The Father' shaped man's identity and image with His words. We must understand how powerful our words are and how even more powerful our silence can be.

Allow me to put a pin right there. In the narrative of the great fall of man, we learned that the serpent was speaking to Eve and Eve to the serpent. Where was Adam? Where was the father that God put in place to keep the garden and rule the world? The Bible places Adam by Eve *("and she gave to her husband, and he did eat"* **Genesis 3**), but there isn't any scriptural recording of Adam's dialogue with Eve or even the serpent. His silence was detrimental to the security of the family. **His silence spoke!** And the whole world is still paying for the reverberating effects of his inability to speak up and put a stop to what was going on.

Fathers, we must be the first man to speak over the lives of our children. We must be the first man to convince our daughters that they are beautiful and our sons that they are mighty and strong. Both of them need to know that they are loved with a real, unchangeable, unconditional father's love. The Father must plant the seeds of greatness in his children and water it with positive affirmation all throughout their lives. The father must never stop speaking! As the writer of the Book of Hebrews reminds us that The Father spoke to us and still speaks, maybe through different ways, but he still speaks. We must follow that example to continue to speak over, to and into the lives of our family! We must learn from Adam's failure to speak! The whole family and the world is thrust into chaos when the father refuses to speak.

Most macho men don't speak much. They don't express their feelings too much either. They feel that speaking and an expression of one's feelings is feminine and something that women do. Not so! Men, we must speak. We think we speak through our actions and that's great. But that alone isn't enough. We must speak the seeds of greatness into our families. We must speak up when things aren't right. We must speak out when things are wrong in our spirit. And we must especially speak for and to our children.

God The Father & Jesus The Son
Now I want to focus our attention to the relationship of God the Father and Jesus the Son as it relates to our subject matter.

*I will proclaim **the LORD's decree**: He said to me, "**You are my son;** today I have become your father. **Psalm 2:7***

*"For unto which of the angels said he at any time, **Thou art my Son, this day have I begotten thee?** And again, I will be to him a Father, and he shall be to me a Son?" Hebrews 1:5*

In the Psalms, David is prophetically repeating a conversation that has transpired before the foundations of the world. The Author of Hebrews clearly elucidates and confirms that fact. He also points out that GOD The Father was not talking about David in this Prophetic discourse, he further explains that GOD The Father was refereeing to JESUS the Christ, The Only Begotten Son of GOD.

Once again it is vital to note that, even though JESUS was and is **the only Begotten** Son of GOD; Adam is the Son of GOD by virtue of the fact that GOD created, made, formed and informed Him. The difference between the two, is that Christ, JESUS was not made by GOD, He was born of GOD. The full substance of Christ was GOD Himself and not from any created matter, therefore, as the Apostles declared, Jesus was able to carry "the fullness of GOD", for He proceeded from the fullness of GOD. As great as Jesus was, the Father still saw it necessary to pro[claim] and declare Him as HIS Son.

Of course, Christ would have known that GOD was His father, and all the heavenly host would affirm him to be so, just by virtue of the similitude of His nature to His Father's. No different than a good friend or family member knowing the father of a child and declaring to the child: "you look just like your Father"; "you sound just like your father"; "you act just like your father" or "handled that just like your father would". Depending on the lad's perspective of his father, this could very well be a positive affirmation. But it was not the responsibility of the Angels, the created beings or any other voice to speak over JESUS and proclaim His identity; it was the sole responsibility of The Father, just as it is with us. As fathers, we must speak, remember we're the official Speaker of the House.

The father's speech on behalf of, or over his children, shapes identity, protects, affirms, validates and manifests when done consistently and positively. The prophetic declaration will rise! However, the lack of speech confuses, leaves questions, causes discord and just hurts. In God's declaration of His Son, He claimed him (HIS SON) to himself. He took ownership of Jesus and this announcement was not just for the Son as much as it was for all things, even things yet to be created. This proclamation was and is recorded throughout time and space so that all will come to know who God's Son is and whose God's Son is! So again, in the proclaiming, there was a claim! There was a seeding into the identity which said, "That's my boy!"

When a father speaks that line, I don't care how old or young you are; you feel the surge of energy flowing through your body. The sense of self-worth, the feeling of self-confidence, the warmth of validation is unfathomable. Just as with God the Father and God the Son, so as Man the father and man the son. This doesn't just have a rippling effect on the son but it **<u>also has a lasting effect on the daughter.</u>** For the daughter draws from the image of the father to compose her picture of a man and she will then search for that man to marry when she grows up. We will deal more with this subject in chapter five.

What happens when the father is not there? Who does the son draw his manhood from? Who does the daughter draw her first portrait of a man from? The sad reality is the question is still unanswered because that absent father rejected or ignored the call to fatherhood. Our sports heroes, Hollywood stars, superstar singers and performers, our neighborhood "hoodrats" and abusive predators take the place in the lives and hearts of those looking for and asking, **"Where is my father?"** and "Who will speak up for me?"

Jesus knew his father was with him and because of that he knew who He was as a person! Why? Because the father made sure of that from the beginning of beginnings and the beginning of his life here on earth as well as his earthly ministry. Not only did the father speak, but the son listened and obeyed. It was from that place of obedience that kept the father close to the son in words and deeds. Because the son kept the father's words, it didn't matter how far apart the two of them were, they were one on so many levels, particularly through the words spoken, kept and obeyed.

After being baptized, JESUS came up immediately from the water; and behold, the heavens were opened, and he saw the Spirit of GOD descending as a dove and lighting on Him, and behold, a voice out of the heavens said, <u>*"This is My Beloved Son, in whom I am well-pleased.*</u>*" Mathew 3:16-17*

Look at this! GOD once again speaks over his son, giving him now, not just identity but validation and affirmation thus reflecting on to him a positive self-image! Notice that this is before He performs his first recorded miracle, before his first recorded demonic exorcism and before his first official proclamation. GOD The Father, not only speaks over but He speaks up and for The Son. GOD, The Father, affirms him and validates him thus closing the gap of any need of JESUS to seek any other's approval. GOD ensures His confidence within himself. There was no need for JESUS to work to prove Himself, now He's free to simply fulfill His destiny!

How many of us are working just for approval, just so an authority can say well done, good job? Inside are we transposing that authority to represent our fathers who may not have ever said 'good job?' 'I'm proud of you; you're awesome!' Jesus was given the "thumbs-up" at every stage of his life as it relates to his interaction with this world.

When GOD The Father commanded the light (The Son) That shined in Genesis, He stepped back and said "it was good". GOD The Father threw a heavenly party at His Son's earthy entrance into the world, the angels sang "peace on earth". And at the birthing of Jesus's public ministry, GOD the Father said "I'm well pleased". Again, GOD took ownership of JESUS, as his son but did not steal His praise.

Sometimes fathers can steal the credit from their children. They themselves may need to be healed from their own father issues. GOD The Father does the complete opposite. <u>He claims the Son but at the same time, He praises the Son.</u> **<u>JESUS in return claims the Father and praises the Father</u>**. What a beautiful exchange. See, when you know who you are, you have no problem complimenting or giving credit to someone else. <u>You're not in competition, you're in destiny.</u>

JESUS was so sure of who He was, that He said (in John chapter 5), that He didn't even need the testimony of man to bear witness of who was and is. When He perceived that the people wanted to make him king by force, (For their own agenda.) He pushed them away, because He already knew that He was The King of Kings and The Lord of Lords, why? That's right His Daddy Told Him! My fellow fathers, what have we told our sons and daughters that would protect them against users and abusers and those who would take advantage of their low self-esteem and poor self-image? Remember the father is the speaker of the House! So Please, Speak!

Where Is My Father?

GOD, The father, spoke so well, so much and so powerful that JESUS didn't even feel the need to make of himself a great reputation as recorded in *Philipians Chapter two*. The source of pride and ego in some cases can come from low self esteem and poor-self image. That can become the root of narcissism and conceitedness. Those who suffer from such, may not be trying to show out and show off as much as they may be trying to prove to themselves that they are somebody. This is something that the father should have done. He should had proved the case that they were somebody simply because they are his children. I often tell my children and remind my siblings that we are great, because we are Robinsons; It's in our blood! Same with you. This self confidence freed JESUS to be about his mission, His service, His purpose and not His reputation. His reputation grew organically because He was focused on his assignment.

How many children and adults are lost on the road of destiny going the wrong way because they're too busy chasing man's approval, recognition and name branding as opposed to walking in the true calling and purposes of God in their lives? How many players are promiscuous not for the love of sexual relations but the sense of validation they derive from it? How many people today are working in the wrong career but are there for the money because the money buys them a sense of false self-worth? None of the above will ever be par to the spoken word of a father over their lives.

A true son will always rise to the prophetic declaration of the father. Notice I didn't say expectations? Sometimes we can put false expectations on our children. A lot of that comes from us trying to live our lives through them and we, every so often think that our children are our second chance at life. That's wrong! We must see the hand of the Lord on their lives and speak to that which God has called them to be with a heart of positive expectation and watch them rise to hit the mark of the spoken word over them! Again the father is the speaker of the house! But if he's not speaking who is?

Chapter Five

Daddy's Girl:

The father in the life of his daughter

We have pretty much focused on the father as it relates to his sons. Though every son needs his father, daughters need him just as much if not more. One could easily make the mistake that because the daughter is a girl, she needs her mother more. After all, the mother can relate better being that they are of the same gender. However, I beg to differ. The roles fathers play in the lives of their daughters are paramount.

A Young Man's Journey Towards A Positive Self-image

It is so necessary that we consider the first male relationship the daughter will have is with her father. Even if the father is absent, it is still the establishment of her male interactions. In our previous chapter, we spoke of how important the father's speech in the house is, well let's revisit that with a huge exclamation point! The father helps to shape the rest of his daughter's life. She is given the model that will most likely follow her for the rest of her life. It is from that image that all her male relationships will be manifested. The father must be her first! He must be the first man she loves and then establish what love is, how it feels, how it sounds and so on. When a father loves, and shows love to his daughter, (please allow me to pause right there) notice I said "love and show love" - remember the chapter that we dealt with the father being the speaker of the house?

It's not enough for the father to just love his daughter, he must show his love to the daughter and articulate that love. He must point out in no uncertain terms what love is and what love is not. When a father loves his daughter, he loves her first-of-all because of who's she is, "she is his daughter." She doesn't have to do anything to earn or keep it. She is and will always be daddy's girl. No matter how old or young, how bad or good, how pretty or not, she's daddy's girl. It is from him that she learns unconditional love from a man! From that knowledge, she is equipped to know the difference between love and attraction, love and affection, and most importantly, love from lust. Without the father being the first man his daughter loves and is shown love, she runs the risk of attempting to find love in all the wrong places.

She may put herself in compromising or dangerous positions because she's trying to find something almost impossible to find in any other relationship other than that of a father. Players and those who mean her no good will use that against her! And the sad thing is that all of it could be avoided if the Father was her first love! She would learn that love and sexual activity are two different things. She would also know that her father loves her without any elicit activity going on. Furthermore, she would know that it could happen. A man can love you without going to bed with you. Then she would be able to decipher a man that loves her from a man that only loves her body. Why? Because her father loved her without touching her inappropriately!

There are some women that feel they must give their body to a person to show love. They are even told that a man wants her body so he can show her how much he loves her. But when the father is the first love, they have the most beautiful relationship by expressing love back and forth in a clean and pure way. This frees her to be able to discern a man's motive and perceive his heart before opening the Pandora's Box of sexual activity. Of course, passions will be there for the man with whom she enters a love connection with. Of course, there is a difference between the love a man and woman shows from the love between a father and daughter. But at least, the core foundation would be established of what love is in its purest and natural form.

I must also share how you interact with her mother will determine how she interacts with a man in a relationship. You are the guide to how she will ultimately be treated. If you don't teach her, no doubt she would have to learn from maybe another male figure or worse. Sometimes life is the most painful and expensive teacher! Men, we must not allow any of the negatives I have stated to happen. We must return to the image of God, so our daughters see God The Father and not just a God since they will automatically idolize us.

She needs to see a righteous man, a holy man, a man of integrity, a man of standard, a man of character. Whatever she sees, she will look for that in her life. You want her to find a good man, so model a good man before her. You want her to find a faithful husband that would honor, cherish and respect his wife, then model that kind of husband before her and you will never have to fight the man she chooses because she will automatically look for a man like you!

Sometimes it's easy to tell when a woman has grown up without a father. A lot of times depending on the circumstances of her father's absence and how the mother represented what he was, they could either be bitter towards men, thinking all men are worthless or think men are great heroes, sacrificing their lives for what they believe. Sadly, it is most commonly true, that when a girl grows up without her father or any positive male figures in her life, they grow up with a learned sense of independence and sometimes an indifference towards authority, especially headship authority. I know I'm about to lose my female readership! But I do believe according to the Bible, that the man is the head of his house. That doesn't mean I believe in chauvinism or that women are sub-human or less than. It simply means to me that the man should cover his house and be responsible for his household members.

"But if any provide not for his own, and especially for those of his house, he hath denied the faith and is worse than an infidel." 1 Timothy 5:8,

"He must manage his family well and see that his children obey him and he must do so in a manner worthy of full respect." 1 Timothy 3:4,

Look at the first scripture. This is saying a man that does not cover his household needs is worse than an unbeliever! Wow! It even goes on to say that he has denied the faith. That is, his life is in direct contradiction to what the Holy Scriptures teaches. God is for family. He's about men taking responsibility for themselves and their families.

Now let's look at the second scripture. Paul is outlining the requirements of an overseer for the church. He equates an overseer to a Husband/Father. He uses his home life as a pre-requisite to the man's ability and right to serve in this capacity of religious affairs. The Apostle Paul puts it right out there! You can't govern the house of God if you can't handle the governance of your house!

Let's focus on our point. Look at how God positions the man. When Jesus was teaching his disciples, he urged them not to Lord over the flock of God, but to feed them, cover them, protect them and guide them. And God through the Apostle, connects this to what a father does for his family. He doesn't lord over them. But as a loving protector that covers, leads, guides and provides. The only issue is when a woman has grown up without a father she may not know what it is to obey a father or rather obey authority, especially male authority. This will be a great strain on any relationship she has with authority, not just authority between husband and wife, but employer and employee, police and community, judge and people. It's at home from daddy that she learns to respect this kind of authority, especially male authority.

One of the most important things for a man is RESPECT. No man wants to be disrespected, especially in his home. This is learned based on how the father and daughter deal with each other and how the mother/wife deals with the father/husband in front of the kids. I know we are focusing on the Father, but most daughters eventually become mothers. So, it's a cycle. In order to stop the vicious cycle of dysfunction and brokenness, we must start with daddy's little girl.

Fathers, we must live respectably and honorably, warranting the due reverence from every household member.

"Fathers do not provoke your children to anger by the way you treat them. Rather, bring them up in the discipline and instruction that comes from the Lord." Ephesians 6:4 NLT

If we must say, "we are the man," "we are the head," "we are the father"; something is wrong or off. We should not need to reaffirm who we are but rather we should be able to affirm each member of our household! We must not provoke them to anger! Be the example that God calls us to be to our daughters so that they will grow up in God and look for a Man of God!

Remember, you must be the first man to tell them they are beautiful, you must be the first man to tell them they are smart and you must be the first man to tell them "I love you." The Father must build their confidence and their self-esteem. **He becomes their glasses by which all men are seen through**. So, be there for them to oversee, guide and provide for every stage of their life! Be their first date, show them how a man should open the door, pull out the chair and cherish their company. Be their first fan at their plays or recitals. When you have done your job well, as you walk them down the aisle of Holy matrimony, you and you alone will have the honor and position to give your baby away to the man that will love, cherish, hold and respect her all her life just like you have! That moment when you look into her eyes and you release her from your covering into the tent of another, you have hope because you have been a model example! But remember, at the end of the day, no matter what, she will always be daddy's girl!

{Let's check in on Earnest and see how he's making out on his journey.}

A Young Man's Journey Towards A Positive Self-image

The Pages of My Life

I Found a Way to Kill Earnest

Going to church for me was like entering another world! There, I would hear people refer to each other with different names, like "Sister" this and "Brother" that. The names got better, like "Deacon", "Minister", "Elder", "Pastor" and "Bishop". They were all dressed up! Happy! Joyful! And, on their grind! They were somebody! They were esteemed! They were loved! Yes, they were awesome. Outside of the church some of them were single parents, poor, minimum wage workers, but in the church, they mixed right in with whole families, rich folk, bosses and "shot callers" (I hope I said that right). There was no difference! They were all in the same boat! And all somebody special!

The lightbulb went off! Maybe God was not bad at all! Maybe he loved us so much that he gave us another world to escape from this world of pain, hurt and defeat. I made up my mind that I wanted God and I wanted to be in this world! I would hear preachers often say, to be in the spirit you had to die to your flesh. I didn't know what it all meant but I did hear that I had to die! That was my chance; I could kill myself! I could kill Earnest! Yes, and become who? Well, I didn't know that yet, I was seven! But at least half of my problem was solved! Earnest was going to die!

One day in church, I was acting out in children's church and my mother grabbed me and began to take me upstairs. I knew for sure that Mommy knew I was being bad and the teachers were having a problem getting me to settle down. I was most certain that she came to "bless my soul" if you know what I mean. If you don't, that meant to give me a good spanking. As I walked on my tippy toes and she grasped tightly on my arm, I began to confess, thinking if I tell on myself maybe she'll have mercy on me.

A Young Man's Journey Towards A Positive Self-image

So, I asked, are you going to spank me because I kept getting out of my seat? (No answer). Are you going to spank me because I kept shouting out at the teacher? (No answer). Are you going to spank me because I kept pinching the girl's butts? (This was a big one, but no answer). I asked, "Well what did I do? Why are you going to spank me?" Still no answer and by this time, we were upstairs in the main auditorium of the church! She said to the Pastor (Supt. Robert L. Madison) "Save him before I kill him!" (I thought to myself, "Hey I wasn't alone, mommy wanted to kill Earnest too") but he took me and lead me to Christ! That night I could partake in Holy Communion, a rite only for saved believers. What an honor!

The next week on Mother's Day, we threw a party for mommy at our house despite our family woes. While she was thanking us, I began to experience the power of God moving in my belly. She looked at me and said "I know you feel it because I feel Him too!" Well, I was off! I burst out in tongues, (called the baptism of the Holy Ghost with the evidence of speaking in an unknown tongue). I would continue to speak and stay in the spirit for almost two hours. Afterward, God revealed some things to me and gave me a special message for all my family members in the house. I didn't know it then, but that was the beginning of my prophetic ministry. To me, Earnest was dying! The only problem was I was still called that Special Ed faggot! I would have to come up with a better plan, a better solution.

Eventually, mommy would move us to Long Island, New York. For her, it was a better place to raise a family. Thank God she did! I could still remember getting chased down the block and up the stairs of our house in the projects. We went to sleep to the sound of sirens, music and gunshots all night, every night. In Long Island, it was peaceful, quiet, and beautiful. We had grass! I had never seen grass like that, it was a lawn! A driveway! Wow! This was awesome!

A Young Man's Journey Towards A Positive Self-image

After searching for a new church home, God would direct our steps to a small church in Brentwood, in the pastor's basement. It was there that God would reveal his calling for me to preach the gospel of Jesus Christ. As I got up to testify, the preacher observed my presentation. When he got up, he said, "I know that God is on that boy! He's a preacher! Bring him up here with me, (he was in the pulpit) I am going to make him a minister!" Wow! Three things happened for me that day!

<u>1. I was called to preach the gospel!</u>
<u>2. I found a father!</u>
<u>3. Best of all, I could finally kill Earnest!</u>

Going home that night, I gathered my brothers and sisters and broke the news to them! They were excited for me until I told them they had to call me "Minister Robinson." I could still remember my two sisters saying, "Jr. please! We're not calling you Minister Robinson!"), so then I tried to negotiate with them saying, "Ok call me Minister Jr." They both refused and at the time, I really didn't know why it was so important for them to call me Minister

Where Is My Father?

Robinson. But it was my way of escaping the horrors of Earnest. I was reborn; I was given a new name in my church world. I would continue to live in that church world in all areas of my life. I was not Earnest. I was Minister Robinson, then Elder Robinson, then Prophet Robinson, then Pastor Robinson and now Bishop Robinson. As I grew up in my new world, I also moved into what I knew was my destiny. The only problem was that broken little boy was still broken and looking for his father. The positions changed, the title changed, but the pain remained the same. If anything, it just grew greater and greater.

For a brief moment as a teenage preacher, Minister Robinson was alive, and Earnest Jr. was dead. All was well in life! I found a way to kill Earnest for good or so I thought. For now, Minister Robinson was in charge. Now I could look at my pastor and mimic him, copy him and study him. Now I had a male role model. Now I had a man that could show me how to be a man, even if it was only in the

A Young Man's Journey Towards A Positive Self-image

church. Now I had a father! He had a son and his name was Minister Robinson.

I thought I was in a position to work and earn the love of God and from my "new father". I could work to earn the respect of my family and those around me. Now, they couldn't call me Special Ed faggot. They had to call me Minister Robinson. They couldn't call me gay. Now they had to call me Minister Robinson. I would be respected, I would be honored and I would be loved! And boy did I preach! Now through all this craziness, the Hand of God was truly on me! At twelve years old I was preaching like a grown man! And I told it like it was!

It was like in this church world I was somebody; in the other world I was nobody. I liked myself in this church world. My image in this world was awesome! I liked what I saw. I liked who I was and I liked who I was becoming! I was special, a 12-year-old preacher! Yeah, that's special! That's awesome! That's powerful! Earnest was dead and the great young prodigy was alive! He was coming *with the thunder! Minister Robinson was my train ticket headed toward a positive self-image! So I thought...*

Chapter Six

My First Hero Called Dad!

Fathers in the lives of their sons

I really don't have to spend a lot of time here because the whole concept of this book deals with fathers and sons. However, I wanted to utilize this chapter to emphasize a few key points with respect to the necessity of a son looking up to the father. If you are a son, this chapter is just for you.

Jesus stated, everything He did, he saw His Father Do. David encouraged King Solomon to hear and neglect not the instructions of His Father. Remember, man was made in the very image of The Father. Lastly, Jesus said when you see ME; you see THE FATHER. Now as my son would say, "let's see how this works".

The Father is and ought to be the son's first superhero. At first, the father is invincible, all powerful and just the greatest. The son sees the father from a distant place. The son sees the father on a pedestal that he himself could never reach. That makes him his superhero because the father can do what the son cannot in his own mind. However, when the father takes his son along, for the ride of greatness and shows him that they are both one and the same. He reveals to the son, the notion "that, if I can do it, so can you". From this interaction, the father moves from a place of incomparability in the eyes of the son, to an object of reflection. Continued time spent with the father develops the seeds of greatness sown into the son, as well as plays a vital role in his maturity.

The father becomes the silent image of identity for the son. The son looks to the father and draws from that vision, his self-image. The father knowing this, works with his son's desire to be like him but shifts the direction from being *like* him to being *greater than* him. Every father wants his son to succeed him, exceed him and surpass him. Even Jesus wanted his disciples to do greater works than him.

Since the father and son share the same blood and the life of the flesh is in the blood, there are like passions, likeness and shared character traits. Who better to help the son mature into the man of purpose, then the father who had to mature himself? The son is only looking at a father who has been a son. The father is simply looking at a son who is yet to be fathered and matured. That creates an atmosphere of both hope and anticipation. Hope, because the son can become mature, great and awesome like his dad. The father can expect greatness from the son. Remember, we touched on when God the Father declared *"that this is my beloved son (Jesus) in whom I am well pleased with."* Keep in mind that Jesus had not begun his earthly work. He was actually being baptized so that he could be released into his public ministry. How can the father be so proud of the son before the son really does anything significant? Through hope and anticipation! The mere fact that Jesus had grown in stature, wisdom and in favor with God and man, was enough for the Father to be proud. There's nothing more awesome than a father watching his son growing up to be the man he always knew he could be. Responsible! Dependable! Great! Wise! Mature and Holy! He (the Son) started growing in the direction of the father then somewhere along the way he becomes his own man! Never will he lose the imprint of the fathers' hand, but he becomes great in his own right.

Fathers help to shape the identity of the sons. They pull on the strings of purpose until destiny takes over. Once the father sees that destiny has stood up in the life of their sons and they know that they have done everything they could to prepare the sons' character, heart, mind and soul for it, at that very moment, the father can stick out his chest and pound away with pride and joy because he knows that his son has just stepped into greatness! He doesn't even have to be there to the very end to see it all come together, at the beginning of the "destiny take over", the father knows without a shadow of doubt that the son is ready! The son is great! The Son is A MAN!

I believe in all my heart that's what God The Father saw in Jesus, The Son. Destiny had come to take Jesus into his purpose and Jesus was ready! For that, God was pleased (not just pleased but "well pleased")!

What did God's expressed pleasure do for Jesus?

        1. It **validated** HIM
        2. It **affirmed** HIM
        3. It **identified** HIM

Fathers, we must remember the above stated and highlighted words are so vital to the success of sons. With that, the son is free from having to spend his life looking for it and wasting precious time resolving or trying to get it, because he had it from the beginning. Now the son can focus his attention on fulfilling his purpose and not the purposes of others in hopes of getting what his father should have given to him from the start of his journey. The big three (validation, affirmation and identification) were key while he was in the wilderness to be tempted of the devil. **(Matthew the 4th Chapter)** Let's revisit that story line.

The devil asked HIM to do key things that would confirm who HE was. That is, if in fact HE was the Son of God. Therefore, the **Big Three** made sure that Jesus had a positive self-image before being tempted. He was secure in who he was and not lured into the temptation of proving himself to his hater, The devil. The very act of proving himself to satan could have cost him the mission. Jesus had to be sure of who He was in order to stay focused on His divine assignment.

How many of us are distracted by the temptation of proving ourselves to people? Most of these people don't like us and never will because of what they already know about us. I am speaking of our potential. If we don't know who we are, we're left open for prey to those who feast on our low self-esteem, poor self-image and insecurities. Jesus would have killed Himself or at the very least put His life in danger, had He fallen into the trap of proving Himself to the devil.

How did he avoid the trap? Well, in addition to the Father serving as the Speaker of the House, like we covered in chapter four; Remember the Father gave him the big three! Fathers, we must give our sons the big three so no one can take advantage of them. It's their secret weapon against folks like that. Once more, it's my understanding, that the "temptation" was not to sin as much as it was satan tempting Jesus to prove himself. But again God, The Father, already did that.

Fathers, we give our sons a fighting chance to succeed when we give them the Big Three! Again, they are <u>Validation</u>, <u>Affirmation</u> and <u>Identification</u>.

After Jesus came from the wilderness, He worked miracles and began to preach the gospel of the Kingdom of God. Remember as we covered in chapter four, as He traveled, a group of people who meant him no good at all said in their hearts; "*We will make him king.*" Sometimes promotions are not for us as much as it is for the person who calls themselves doing the promoting. People will appear to promote you to a place you were already destined to be, but they feel if they promote you, your rise to power or fame is owed to them. If you have the big three, you would know where you're going without needing to be affirmed by others who aren't qualified to do so. Like Jesus, you will be able to perceive their motives and not need their false promotion. Why? The father already gave you the big three from the very beginning. This concept of identity and a positive self-image is so important to real success.

When the son is established in his identity and has a positive self-image, he is in a safe place, others call it secure. A lot of times we don't take the time to really understand insecurities because we are too frustrated by its traits. Simply put, insecurity is a state of feeling unsafe. Unsafe in their various places: place of relationship; place of vocation; place of mental stability; and the place of emotional equilibrium. Understanding One's Self-identity and a Positive Self-image make it very hard to be insecure. As we have discovered, the seeds of identity and a positive self-image are sown into the life of a son by the father.

Remember, the father is the speaker of the house and his words carry weight! Therefore, fathers watch what you say. Our Bible shows us what not to do or say through the story of Noah in **Genesis 9**. *(When he cursed ham, his grandson, for his father's sin).* Your words not only reach your immediate offspring but generations to come.

Be careful not to speak out of anger or frustration. Even God came in the cool of the night to confront Adam and Eve (his first earthly children), when they messed up. There is a thin line between correction and abuse. God could correct Adam and Eve and yet keep from killing them. Sometimes we can kill our son's spirit, their motives and their drive all with the intentions of just correcting a bad decision or inappropriate behavior.

Don't forget that as fathers, our voice carries. After we are long gone, our sons will hear the words spoken to them by us. Make it count! For the most part, the father's words will outlive him and when the father transitions from this life, it is his words that will remain. So again I say, make it count.

His words are weighty, his actions are iconic, his thoughts are vital because our first superhero is our dad!

Chapter Seven

Grandfathers

"They are the sons God has given me here," Joseph said to his father. Then Israel said, "Bring them to me so I may bless them."
Genesis 48:9

"Children's children are a crown to the aged, and parents are the pride of their children."
Proverbs 17:6 NIV

"A good [man] leaves an inheritance to his children's children"...
Proverbs 13:22a

Honestly, I can close this chapter right here. I love it when The Word of God speaks for itself. Let's dig in just a little to bring this out a little more.

After establishing the necessity of the role of the father, we are now pulled to a shift in fatherhood to 'Grandfathering.' We've covered the topic of a man leaving his father's house to build his own house. So where does that leave the father who served his family faithfully? Is he no longer of use? Is his work finished? No! Now I call this time the gravy years! I believe this is the time where his son, (a new father) will need his support. See the Grandfather shifts from being the provider to the supporter. He's there to guide his son into the paths of being a husband and a father. He's there to remind the son that it's ok to be new at this thing called parenting. Remember we talked about the father being the son's hero? It's important to understand that the son still might think his father is a superhero and he cannot measure up. Thus, he might doubt himself and second guess his ability to effectively serve his family. That's when the grandfather steps in and reassures him with his own life's story. He shares with his son the many memories of his beginning years as a father, the mishaps, mistakes, blunders and bloopers as well as the apparent successes and victories. In this way he provides support.

According to our chapter's theme scripture text, the grandfather has a greater role than that! He blesses his grandkids, but, with what?

1. A prophetic declaration over their life.

2. Impartation of wisdom and truth.

3. An example of a Godly man in his elder years which gives them something to look forward to.

Fathers impart truth, but Grandfathers impart wisdom. That is because the truth the father is imparting may be new to him, something he saw, read or learned. But the Grandfather imparts wisdom that comes from life experience.

The Blessings of the grandfather also includes the vital passing down of generational mysteries and the assurance of proper transcription of their family's history.

The grandfather connects the 1st generation to the 3rd generation to help bring perspective to the 4th generation. He helps to make sure the sons know who they are as a people, their struggles, their victories, their failures and their strengths. He serves as the historian of the family.

Lastly, he leaves an inheritance for his grandchildren. I know the first thing we think about when we see that word inheritance is money, estates and precious possessions. However, there is more to it than just those things. **The money will be spent and estates can be seized. Even precious gemstones and heirlooms can be lost, but the heritage of wisdom can only be lost if it's forgotten.** If the grandson listens to the words of his grandfather and keeps them close to heart, their inheritance can never be lost, but passed down from generation to generation. God required the children of Israel to tell the story of their deliverance from Egypt to their children so that every generation after would know who God is and what God has done for their family. In the same way, our grandfathers, fathers and so on must continue to pass down the wisdom, knowledge and understanding to each generation of their family.

The final thing I want to cover on this subject is legacy. A simple definition of legacy; *is something that is left in a will to another.* For us it is also memory that is transported from the past to the present with the intent of being passed on. Grandfathers should live a life so great that even in death, he lives through his generation, into the second generation of his son and lasting even to the third generation that is his grandchildren. What will our grandchildren say of the life we live today? What legacy are we leaving behind?

Now this is what I like about this word legacy, let's look at its origin: It comes from the late 14 century, meaning a "<u>body of persons sent on a mission</u>, "from Old French legatie meaning "<u>**legate's office,**</u> "from Medieval Latin **legatia**, from Latin legatus" meaning **<u>ambassador, envoy</u>**, implies to, "**appoint by a last will**, send as a legate" Sense of" **property left by will**"

"Daddy did you see that?" As my 8 years old son would holler out whenever I would take him golfing and he had a good shot. So, really, did you see that? One of the definitions of legacy was: "Body of persons sent on a mission." Now trade out the words 'body' for the 'sons and 'person' for 'a family' and let's revisit the definition., **"the *sons* of *a family* sent on a mission."** Whew!

"*Your young men will see visions; your old men will dream dreams.*" **Acts 2:17C**. The grandfather's dreams can very well become the mission of the grandson. Scripture tells us that God will speak to us in dreams. So those dreams that God is speaking to the grandfather are the revelations that he shares with his son and the legacy with his son's sons. I'm speaking of God's calling for the family. I believe in family callings. There are great things that God does through families.

The Israel family's mission was to bless humanity with the Savior of the world, Jesus the Christ of God. That was the family's mission and legacy. Father to son, and so on and so on, even to 42 generations! Jesus came through the seed of Abraham, through the lineage of David. Side note to my mothers, sisters and daughters; I am not leaving you out! God used mighty women of God to help bring this forth. There are actually women noted in the genealogical bloodline of Jesus, recorded in the gospels. However, just for the purpose of this book, I am particularly focusing on the sons mainly because the son carries the seeds to the next generation. When God was done with a generation, he stopped seeding it. That means he allowed the last son to die without a male heir, a son or seed. This could mean that the family has served their purpose on earth but when there is still seed (sons) their purpose is alive. Their mission is still alive! Now, wait, there is always an exception to the rule! I told you my mothers, sisters and daughters I didn't leave you out. Well, check this out!

The Daughters of Zelophehad – Marriage of Female Heirs

"Now the chief fathers of the families of the children of Gilead the son of Machir, the son of Manasseh, of the families of the sons of Joseph, came near and spoke before Moses and before the leaders, the chief fathers of the children of Israel. And they said: "The LORD commanded my lord Moses to give the land as an inheritance by lot to the children of Israel, and my lord was commanded by the LORD to give the inheritance of our brother Zelophehad to his daughters. Now if they are married to any of the sons of the other tribes of the children of Israel, then their inheritance will be taken from the inheritance of our fathers and it will be added to the inheritance of the tribe into which they marry; so it will be taken from the lot of our inheritance. And when the Jubilee of the children of Israel comes, then their inheritance will be added to the inheritance of the tribe into which they marry; so their inheritance will be taken away from the inheritance of the tribe of our fathers."

Then Moses commanded the children of Israel according to the word of the LORD, saying: "What the tribe of the sons of Joseph speaks is right. This is what the LORD commands concerning the daughters of Zelophehad, saying, 'Let them marry whom they think best but they may marry only within the family of their father's tribe.' So the inheritance of the children of Israel shall not change hands from tribe to tribe, for every one of the children of Israel shall keep the inheritance of the tribe of his fathers<u>. **And every daughter who possesses an inheritance in any tribe of the children of Israel shall be the wife of one of the families of her father's tribe so that the children of Israel each may possess the inheritance of his fathers.**</u>"

Numbers 36:1-8 NKJV

These daughters were some "B.A.D." *(bold anointed and determined)* sisters! They stood before Moses the Leader and pleaded the case of their family line! It wasn't just about the land, but keeping the name of their father alive! The daughters carried on the mission of the family. So, even if there are no sons, the name can still go on, the work can go on as long as there was a father and a mission and a family that says it's not over for us! We still have work to do!

Here's one more example for my mothers, sisters and daughters. Remember the prophetic promise of God concerning the victory of Christ: **"Your seed (woman) shall bruise his (the serpent-devil) head."**

Of course we know Mary carried that seed! I'm going to leave that for the next book!

Overall we see that the grandfather has a very important role. The part of that role that stands out as my favorite is that he has to cast vision and speak purpose into the lives of his family so that they can catch it and run with it. Therefore, even in his death, he lives through the works of his sons and daughters from generation to generation.

Chapter Eight

The Sacrifices of the Father

"For God (The Father) so loved the world, that HE gave his only begotten son, that whosoever believes in him shall not perish but have everlasting life."
John 3:16

"No greater love than this, than a man lay down his life for a friend."
John 15:13

Often it's not typical for most men to be naturally expressive or talkative, so one may never know how much fathers sacrifice. Once a man, (a good one), is blessed to become a father, his whole mindset changes and he is not living life for himself anymore as much as he is living for his children. He's not working for himself anymore but working for his kids. Men may brag, but fathers silently sacrifice for their children and family. They will work two or three jobs and do heavy amounts of overtime to ensure their family's survival. They take pride in providing! They get joy on special days like birthdays, Christmas and other days where they can bless their family. When they see the look in their children's eyes after receiving a gift from the father, it makes it all worth it. A good father wants his children happy! Safe! Established! They are willing to sacrifice pretty much anything to make that happen.

So many fathers go without to ensure their families have within. They work harder so their children can work smarter. To be a good dad, many times you must sacrifice your ego and pride. There's nothing manly about having a pretend tea party with your daughter in a tutu, but you sacrifice at that moment to spend quality time with her. There is nothing prideful and egotistical about throwing a game for your son to build his confidence, but the sacrifice is worth it when you see that he sees himself as a winner.

Providing for our families is a great sacrifice because if we just had to pay bills that would be easy. What's hard is working long hours and yet coming home to play catch with Jr., have tea with baby girl, then talk and have stimulating conversation with the wife.

See, our job doesn't stop where we physically work. On the jobs, we have a vocation and that pays the bills, but no money can buy quality time with dad. So dad has another job when he gets home, HE must be DADDY! As tired or mentally worn out as he may be, he must muster up more strength and energy to clock in at the most important job of his life, that's right in his home life!

Fathers go without so their families can have within. Many times they are under-appreciated because they don't always broadcast what they do. Mommy is normally more hands on with the kids, so daddy is sometimes seen as the distant provider. Mothers, it's important that you help to let the children know that daddy is working hard for them every day. Even express to them that some of the things and the lifestyle the family has, are because of his hard work.

There is one more area of sacrifice that many fathers may not mention. This may have something to do with the fact that it doesn't look like a sacrifice as much as a cop out. You probably guessed it, that father who sacrifices himself from the family. This whole book is about the son asking, **"Where is my father?"** and we have dealt intensively with the negative effects of his absence. However, there are times that the father has determined he's no good to the family and will sacrifice precious time to go away so that he can get himself together for the family. Sometimes, addictions are so strong that the father is more of a danger to his family than a band of protection. He has to deal forever with the fact that he missed times, days and moments that he would never get back. But he does it for the betterment of the family. He chooses to be absent, to get help, so the family isn't brought down by his habits or demons. I guess what I am saying is that every absent father is not a cowardly father.

And about the ninth hour Jesus cried with a loud voice, saying, Eli, Eli, lama sabachthani? that is to say, **My God, my God, why hast thou forsaken me**? *Matthew 27:46*

Many of us can identify with what Jesus cried out. Who would have thought that the Son of God, would share in our lament?

For a real father to sacrifice himself from the picture, it takes a lot of strength and love for the family. I say to him it's never too late. I pray that things come together in your life so that you can resume the position of being a provider in your family's life.

How many stories are out there where a father traded himself for death to save their loved one, or took the blame and went to jail to spare his child; or exchanged their freedom so their children wouldn't be bound? Other than a father overcoming an addiction or habit that would put the family's welfare at risk, the above were other acts of heroism done on behalf of the security of the family. So again, every absent father is not a cowardly father. Let's not count out the fathers who serve their God, country, their belief or idea and were willing to sacrifice their life, not just for their immediate family, but also their larger family of neighbors and mankind. Let us salute those that even in their absence speak volumes and show our appreciation for their sacrifices.

{It's about that time again, to check in on Earnest. Let's see what progress he's making.

A Young Man's Journey Towards A Positive Self-image

The Pages of My Life

My New World and Old World Don't Want to Play Nice

After becoming a licensed minister over summer vacation, I went to school that fall. When the teacher had us introduce ourselves, I, of course, introduced myself to her and the class as Minister Robinson. I was serious! In my new church world, we never used first names! Earnest will stay dead and now I would never have to hear his name or remember that he ever existed.

Well, my teacher refused! She said clearly, but authoritatively, that she would not call me Minister Robinson. As she looked at my records she said, "I'll call you Earnest. Well now, after being disrespected, I felt it was only right for me to show her how upsetting it was to be called by your first name. So I replied. "Well then, I'll call you Cathy. Hello, Cathy." I stood there just as confident, knowing that this would prove my point and settle the issue. She would see how calling me Minister Robinson was just as in line as her wanting me to call her Ms. Melay. One big issue was that; I was only 12 years old. So, as I sat in the principal's office for insubordination, I had to come up with another plan. I could not be called Minister Robinson, nor could I be called Earnest, so what was I to do? EJ could work and EJ it was. I was armed for the great negotiation. I did, however, try to get the principal to see my point on the Case of Minister Robinson, but eventually I conceded to EJ.

Now the truth is I had no idea that my subconscious put this whole thing together. At 12 years old, I did not know that I killed Earnest. All I knew was that I liked how Minister Robinson felt. He was confident, sure of himself and he was sharp (I would dress in suits and look like a million bucks). As a matter of fact, Minister Robinson was rich while Earnest was poor! Minister Robinson had people looking to see what he would say. Earnest had people looking to mock and make fun. Minister Robinson had the respect of the people; Earnest was the butt of everyone's joke. The church saved my life. It gave me a new identity, a new name and a new personality whom I loved! People loved this person and most of all, God loved this person.

Honestly, I could not believe my school rejected my new self. I was so excited to go back to school. I wanted them to meet him. Even though, I did not get them to call me Minister Robinson; I embodied him. I portrayed him. I was him. No name could stop me! I was a preacher! I lived, dressed,

A Young Man's Journey Towards A Positive Self-image

talked, behaved and carried myself as a preacher. So what, if you called this preacher EJ, as long as you didn't call him Earnest, I was ok!

Again, I didn't realize the hate for myself or my name until I got older. What did you expect? I was only twelve years old. My classmates and school friends gave me a name that I felt was acceptable. Church boy! Preacher boy! That would do. As long as it wasn't faggot or worse, Special Ed faggot. I was happy with that!

All was well with the world. I had a father in my new world, who gave me the big three (an identity, validation and affirmation). He even gave me a new name, Minister Robinson. I had someone to look up to and imitate. Someone to show me what a man was and who would show me how to be a Man of God! I could still remember the time I would sit next to him in the pulpit. In the chairs reserved for ministers! What?! Monday through Friday, I was picked on. I would go to school and be in special education classes. Yet Sundays I was in a seat of honor. Life was getting better. I was the kid preacher! (Even in my hometown.) It was not a shocking site to see me walking down the street with my Bible or briefcase. Ok, I have to share this. Heck, I would ride my bike in a three-piece suit! Lord help this poor kid! It wasn't an act for me. It wasn't a religious show. For me, it was my new life; my salvation, my service, my ability to love myself and be loved! I was Minister Robinson!

Though my church world didn't play well with the rest of the world, I would force it. I made the church world exist in all of my occupied spaces. I was Minister Robinson, not Jr., not Earnest, not Special Ed faggot, not stupid, not the boy with the p.r.o.b.l.e.m. but Minister Robinson. When I wore my 1ˢᵗ clergy collar… What? You couldn't tell me anything! When my Godmother made me my first robe, I was so excited that I wore it backwards! I looked in the mirror and loved what I saw. I was somebody! Why? You guessed it; it's because I was Minister Robinson!

A Young Man's Journey Towards A Positive Self-image

Chapter Nine

The Blessings of My Father

*"Your father's blessings are greater than the
blessings of the ancient mountains,
than the bounty of the age-old hills. Let all these rest
on the head of Joseph, on the brow of the prince
among his brothers."
Genesis 49:26 NIV*

*"By the God of your father who will help you,
And by the Almighty who blesses you
With blessings of the heavens above,
Blessings lying in the deep that couches beneath,
Blessings of the [nursing]
breasts and of the [fertile] womb."
"The blessings of your father
Are greater than the blessings of my ancestors
[Abraham and Isaac]*

Up to the utmost bound of the everlasting hills;
They shall be on the head of Joseph,
Even on the crown of the head of him who was the distinguished one and the one who is prince among (separate from) his brothers."
Genesis 49:25-26 Amp

Wow! What a statement! To any son, this is truth right here! Let's look at it from a few angles. The first being a natural perspective: as we established in the previous chapters. The son lives for the approval of the father and that is of spoken Validation, Affirmation and Identification. We need all three because they're wrapped up in the one which we call 'approval.'

Jesus did the same thing. Look at how John records it in **John 8:28-29** *(KJV)* So Jesus said, "When you lift up the Son of Man, then you will know that I am He, <u>and I do nothing on My own initiative</u>, but I speak these things as <u>the Father taught Me</u>. And He who sent Me is with Me; <u>He has not left Me alone</u>, for I always do the things that are pleasing to Him."

The ultimate root of Jesus' motivation on earth was to please the Father. It was from that starting point that initiated all his works. It was his key inspiration. That was a success for him and apparently HE was successful! We've read this scripture before, **Matthew 3:17** "And behold, a voice out of the heavens said, "This is My Beloved Son, in whom I am well pleased." THE FATHER was very pleased with Jesus. Again the beautiful thing was that THE SON didn't have to earn it. The Father was just pleased in having a son and the son was so pleased with having a father that he worked to please the father until pleasing the father became his work in life. What a tongue twister! Or moreover, pleasing the father was the inspiration of all his works in this lifetime here on earth.

I can identify from that premise; it is natural for a son to seek the approval of the father in that he works to please him. In that pleasure, the father releases approval. How many of us wanted to make the winning shot, or the tackle, or bring home that high grade or the beautiful girl all so that dad would be pleased? Good fathers use this to help push their sons and daughters to be their best. I cannot stress enough that, the Father begins to shape the identity and positive self-image of his children by speaking into their life and spirit.

One of the key definitions of blessed is to be truly happy. So all a good father wants for his children is for them to be truly happy. And to be their best!

Live their best! Act their best! At first, you are doing it for your father's approval. Yet somehow in the process, you learn the discipline of being the best.

Jesus says He – (The Father) has not left Me – (The Son). I think our fathers never leave us. Even if they leave us by location or in this lifetime here on earth, they never leave us in word and spirit (inspiration, motivation). Physically, The Father God and the Son Jesus were light years away but were one spiritually, motivationally, in word and deed. If the proper impartation is made into your sons, you will never leave them even if you have to leave them physically. A part of you will always be with them. You truly can't leave them because they are made of you and from you. With your help, they will become their own person with their own dreams, goals and visions guided by your voice of instruction and the impartation of wisdom that still speaks even in your absence.

This leads us into the next section of this chapter. We already dealt with The Father as the speaker of the house, but I want to revisit that train of thought once again, for this chapter.

If one of the most important driving forces in a son's heart is to please the father, then the father's

blessings are vital to him. It is just as important to his daughters as well, but I want to focus on the son for now.

The Father's blessings are for us as sons the reward for the hard work of the father's pleasure. What is the Father's blessing? In *Genesis,* Jacob makes a powerful statement- the father's blessing is paramount. You can receive honors, praise, titles, positions, money and riches, but if you don't believe your father blesses what you have done, it takes away from your celebration of these accomplishments. Yes, it's that deep. **No matter how good they tell you have done, it doesn't register completely until the father stamps it with his approval.** So here we see Jacob doing what was done for him and his father that is, giving the Official Father's blessing to his sons. What a tradition. Fathers, I beg you, please don't leave this earth without giving your blessings to your son(s). But the question remains: what is the father's blessing?

1. **God**

Yes, God is the first blessings of the Father. The father must introduce his son to the ultimate source of all blessings and that is God himself. He must model the relationship with God before his son. He must instruct him how to enter into HIS presence and how to build a relationship with God. He must give his sons the blessedness of faith. That is the foundation of a spiritual relationship with God.

"And thou, Solomon, my son, know thou the God of thy father, and serve him with a perfect heart and with a willing mind: for the LORD searches all hearts, and understands all the imaginations of the thoughts: if thou seek him, he will be found of thee; but if thou forsake him, he will cast thee off forever."
1 Chronicles 28:9

2. Verbal expression of The Powerful Big Three

Affirmation, Validation and Identification- Remember, wrapped up in one word: Approval! It sounds like this: "I am proud of you son! Good Job! That's great! You are awesome! You have become a great man! You have become a great father! You made something good of yourself! You are the man!" My friend, you have no idea what these words mean to a son!

3. Tangible Property (Inheritance)

A father works to build wealth for his children to build upon. He works so that they will have a better start than him. Let's go back to a part of our opening scripture reference "The blessings of your father 'are' greater than the blessings of my ancestors (Abraham and Isaac).

This speaks about a compounding of wealth. God blessed Abraham; Abraham willed his son those blessings. The Father's blessing goes beyond some property.

Let's stop here for a moment to get your Bible and read the *scripture* **Genesis** *25:5-6.* From these two verses, we learn a few things.

1. The son of the promise (Isaac) received ALL.

2. The sons of the concubine only received a gift. This has great implications. Later in the book, I will cover spiritual fathers and sons. But just to give a quick preview- every spiritual father will have two types of sons: one born from covenant relationship and the other born from the flesh. Both are sons. However, only the covenant born sons can receive ALL from the father whereas the fleshly (carnal mind) born son, could only get gifts. So in both the natural and spiritual realms I encourage you to get it all! Not just the gifts, even though the blessing does encompass the tangible values. The rest of the blessing is not materialistic, instead its character, development and process. Without these, the son will not be able to keep the inheritance left to him. Just as it was with the prodigal son, when he separated himself from the father, he wasted all he had. What took multiple lifetimes to accumulate was wasted in a few days of un-fathered living. What do I mean by "un-fathered"? I mean a lifestyle that rejects the teachings, wisdom and model of the father. King Solomon says in the "the wealth of the sinner is laid up for the just". What does this have to do with a good man leaving an inheritance for his children's children? Everything. How will the inheritance last two generations after him? It isn't a matter of how much money, land and resources the Good Man (father) leaves his son. It's the wisdom, knowledge and understanding that was left that makes the difference. It's that Trinity that will preserve the spiritual inheritance and cause the tangible blessings to remain. It's the teaching of righteousness, true holiness and lifestyle that will cause the God of the Father to be with the son! It's that same God that will bless the son as He blessed the father! But if he sins and lives "un-fathered," he can expect the wealth his father left for him to be given to another. God will make the transfer.

4. <u>Prophetic Word Spoken over Their Life</u>

The Father has the divine right to speak over their life, into their life and for their life. God honors, the words of the father!

"And Jacob called unto his sons and said; Gather yourselves together, that I may tell you what which

shall befall you in the last days. Gather yourselves together, and hear, ye sons of Jacob, and hearken unto Israel your father." *Genesis 49:1-2*

This passage of scripture in the King James Version of the Bible is labeled: Jacob Blesses His Sons. Isn't that powerful? I'm sure Jacob spoke over the lives of his sons their whole life. But this time is different because it's close to his death and this is a blessing that would carry them into their destiny. He will not be there in person, but his "Last Will", shall abide with them in *Word* and *Spirit* forever. This is crucial and is recorded in the Heavens and Earth. Father's words carry you throughout your entire lifetime and must be spoken again for the next generation. How do I know that these words were spoken and recorded in both *natural* and *spiritual* realms? He used both names. Their father had two names, A. Natural: Jacob and B. Spiritual: Israel. Jacob was his natural name given by his parents. Israel was his spiritual name given by God who sits in the heavens. He spoke from both places! Therefore, it was recorded in both places.

Fathers, you must speak from both places; the natural and spiritual. In your leisure, read the rest of the chapter in *Genesis 49* and see how what was spoken came to pass. The fathers speak but as a son; we must listen. That declaration can shape or alter our destiny.

5. The Father himself

Let's look at Elisha. *"As they were going along and talking, behold, there appeared a chariot of fire and horses of fire which separated the two of them. And Elijah went up by a whirlwind to heaven. Elisha saw it and cried out, "My father, the chariots of Israel and its horsemen!" And he saw Elijah no more. Then he took hold of his own clothes and tore them in two pieces."* 2 Kings 2:11-12

Even though we are going to dig deeper into this in the coming chapters, let me just illustrate the brokenness of *Elisha* when he saw *Elijah* being taken from him. It's like the scene of a child being taken from their parents, kicking, screaming and crying hysterically. That child doesn't know to be upset because of tangible things. Rather it is the breaking away from the presence of their parents that rips them apart. Even Jesus experienced this on the cross, when he cried out to The Father, and asked why God forsook Him. **Only true sons value the father more than gifts and resources**.

To those true sons, the Father is the Blessing. Just as with Abraham, God was the reward and everything else fails in comparison to the love, attention and presence of a father. Memories with a dad will outlast the most valued possessions. But when our father is taken up or transcends this life, we still have him. We have him in his words, his teachings and wisdom in our memories. So make every moment you have with your father count. Whether you are on the porch of a shack or the entry way of a mansion, things disappear when in the presence of a father, your father.

So fathers, please understand your presence is the greatest gift you can give to your son and the most expensive thing you can take away. When I say presence I mean attention, the deliberate determination to be active and attentive to your son's and daughter's life. That for me is presence. Don't be there in body but not in spirit. Be there! If you are there, be there! For this could never be understated or underestimated.

We spoke about the five blessings for the son; now I will share one blessing with the father.

"And Abram said, Behold, to me thou hast given no seed: and, lo, one born in my house is mine heir."
Genesis 15:3

The Blessing of the Father is A Son! Now I'm not speaking just about gender; I am focusing on the fact that God's gift to men is the divine right to fatherhood! Another one of the blessings of the father is a seed. That's a blessing because the seed reproduces itself. The seed represents a son because the son carries the seed within him. He will then cast that seed and reproduce himself into the next generation.

<u>We can see that there are two blessings here:</u>
1. God blesses us to be a natural father for children we have reproduced.
2. If God gives us a male child, he is considered a seed for the next generation.

Even if we are only given the first; being a father alone is awesome. So we close this chapter with the blessings of the father manifested in both likes: in that the children get a daddy and the man gets the gift of fatherhood! He goes from being just a man to being a Father!

Chapter Ten

Stepping Back into Place:

Re-establishing a relationship with your father

from a broken connection

"And all things are of God, who hath <u>reconciled us to himself</u> by Jesus Christ, and hath given <u>to us the ministry of reconciliation</u>; To wit, that God was in Christ, reconciling the world unto himself, <u>not imputing their trespasses unto them</u>; and hath committed unto us the <u>word of reconciliation</u>." 2 Corinthians *5:18-19*

By now you already know and appreciate the need for a father and a positive relationship with him. You understand how his effective role in your life is to your benefit. But, maybe you (like me) question, "How do I re-establish a relationship with my father from a broken one? As my son, EJ would say, "I know exactly how you feel." One of the things you have to do is look past the brokenness. Focusing on brokenness forces you to relive the pain, the hurt and the rejection and of course walk in un-forgiveness. Those things will never let you move past them to focus on reconciliation. From that perspective, you have to give up too much, for reconciliation and from that point of view, the relationship might not be worth giving up so much negativity for.

According to scripture our sins have alienated us from our God *(Colossians 1:21)*. We are not just alienated as a form of separation, as in different regions or different locale but also our sinful ways and thoughts have made us enemies of GOD Himself. It's one thing to be separated, but it's a totally different thing to be enemies. However, God loved us so much and wanted to restore His Father-child relationship with us. So he did something about it! In short, HE did three very powerful things:

1) **He Forgot** – "I even I, am he who blots out your transgressions for my own sake, and <u>**remembers your sins no more**</u>." *Isaiah 43:25*

2) **He Forgave** – "He is faithful and just to **<u>forgive</u>** us our sins..." *1John 1:9*

3) **He called us unto himself** – "But ye are a chosen generation, a royal priesthood, a holy nation, a peculiar people; that ye shew forth the praises of him who hath **<u>called</u>** you out of the darkness into his marvelous light; Which in time past *were not a people*, but are now the people of God: which had not obtained mercy, but now have obtained mercy." *1 Peter 2:9-10*

<u>1st - God Forgot</u>

The Prophet Micah declared that God casts our sins into the sea forgetfulness! Wow! God purposely forgot our sins! He took it off and out of His Mind so he can see us through the eyes of love and not vengeance or wrath.

If we are going to restore a broken relationship with our fathers, we must start with letting go of the past! Honestly, we can't go back in time. We only have today. We must purposefully forget in order to get what we want, which is a healthy relationship with our father. At this point, you may be calling me crazy and throwing this book on the floor. I don't blame you. It's crazy, but true! We must forget yesterday so we can enjoy today.

What does that look like? Did God completely forget everything regarding our sins? That's a question for HIM to answer. But what I know he did do was decide not to hold it against us, charge us or dwell on it! Choose not to live in the thoughts of the pain, hurt, abandonment, abuse and rejection of our past time with our father! **Choose to live in the now**. It is in the now- here in the present- that you will help to make better. Yesterday is Gone. Let's follow our heavenly father's example through all our hurtful thoughts and experiences with our fathers. What we consider sins they have committed against the relationship especially, must be cast out into the sea of forgetfulness!

You may ask, Earnest, if God needed a sea to cast his thoughts of our sins to prevent him from remembering it; what do I do with all my hurtful and painful thoughts of my past with my father so that I can move towards a positive relationship with him?

> "Cast your cares on the LORD
> and he will sustain you;
> He will never let the righteous be shaken,"
> Psalms 55:22

When we cast all those thoughts onto the Lord He will lift the burden and provide us with the freedom from the weight we are carrying from our past. He will also sustain you in your healing process if you tell Him all about it. Another translation of that very same text literally says **"cast your burdens…"** Our cares can very well become burdens! If we trust God, and allow him, He will carry them, then we can unload all that hurt, pain, rejection, abandonment, abuse and anger. All of this is necessary for re-establishing a relationship and busting open the doors that are blocking you. **So decide today, I will forget to be mad!** I will forget to get even! I gave it to God to work it out!

2nd – God Forgot to Forgive

God was able to forgive us freely because he forgot the pain and hurt of our sin! If we could forget the pain of our past regarding our relationship with our father, that would make forgiveness a whole lot easier. To forgive is to release from the resentment, the penalty and the debt! It's hard to forgive when we feel like they haven't paid the price for our pain yet! We are afraid that they will get off easy and not suffer like us! So when we forgive, we've canceled the debt of pain, hurt and loss we experienced by their hand and release them from having to pay for it. What an awesome example we have in God. God was not at fault! He didn't sin against our relationship with him and he still paid the price for the sin we committed. He loved us so much and wanted to restore the relationship so badly!

> *"[For] God so loved the world that he*
> *[gave] His only begotten son,*
> *that whosoever believed in Him shall not perish*
> *but have everlasting life."*
> *John 3:16*

Notice the first word in this text is "**For**" and the ninth is "**gave**". Yes, **forgave** is the operative word. Remember in our definition of father, we deal with him being the first. So God the Father was first to forgive. Nine is the number of birthing; it is also the number of judgment. God loved us so much that he forgave us. He paid the judgment needed to birth a new relationship with us.

> *"For if ye forgive men their trespasses,*
> *your heavenly Father will also forgive you:*

> *But if ye forgive not men their trespasses, neither will your Father forgive your trespasses."*
> <u>Matthew 6:14-15.</u>

If you ever need help forgiving someone, just remember, God forgave you! Knowing this now gives you the opportunity to be free to forgive and live without fear!

Note, forgiving doesn't relieve you from the emotional pain and heartbreak right away, but it does release you from it. That is, it no longer has a title deed on you! There will be times when you will have to remind yourself that you forgave and forgot! Why? Because when something comes up and it tries to remind you of the pain, that pain is trying to wake up wrath and anger. However, you must continue to stand up and remind all your members; you don't want to [**re**]member that because you already decided to forget! Don't let those moments reattach to your "now" because you [**dis**]membered it from your life and heart when you forgot it.

3rd - He Recalled Us Unto Himself!

According to the Apostle Peter, God called "a people" unto Himself who weren't even His people by virtue of Abraham's Promise. The people He called did not have a direct covenant with God; not for God to remember or be held accountable for. However, there was a universal promise that pre-dated Abraham's promise that is sandwiched between the women's judgment and the serpent's judgment in *Genesis.* Precisely, in *Genesis 3:15* God promised to send a deliverer to set the human race free from the power of the serpent!

Mankind was thrust into darkness by Adam and Eve's decision to disobey God, therefore we as mankind sinned. We messed up, but God came through His Son, by way of Mary (a virgin) and produced a seed (male child) who defeated Satan forever! Glory to God in the Highest and Peace on Earth! This price was paid by the ultimate sacrifice. The Father sacrificed His Only Son that He might return to himself, his children called mankind *(John 3:16).*

Now that was not enough for God to stop there, he didn't leave us there. Where was there? It is a place of forgiveness. He went even further. He called us back to him. There is also a place of full reconciliation. Furthermore, there is the place where God the Father re-instated the relationship!

He said, yes you hurt me, but I forgave you and I forgot about it purposely. Now I am coming to tell you it's alright, let's just be friends again. WOW! I am getting happy here!

So just like God the Father, we must follow that same example. **We must Forget. We Must Forgive. We must Recall.** Remember, God has given us the ministry and word of reconciliation. I say to the son, if your father is still alive, Go! Go Now! Cast all your hurtful thoughts and list of burdens to God your heavenly Father, then forgive your father for not being there. Take initiative and you can recall the relationship. How?

1. You reach out! Yes, you! In recalling the relationship, don't try to make him make up for lost time. Time has passed and you will never get it back. But you can have today.
2. Reach out without expectations. Yes, reach out without looking for anything but a relationship.
3. Start from today and make today great! Start out with a deep desire to have a relationship and allow the relationship to develop into what it should be.

4. Don't try to force it. Remember it will be tough; you will have apprehension and concerns, but remember to walk in Faith, not fear!
5. Start as friends, get to know one another. Build trust, spend time and build communication.
6. Don't just talk about the past and the pain of yesterday. Talk about today. From there you have a springboard that the both of you can leap from into a greater depth of relationship.
7. Remember, throw your list of hurts and pain into the heart of God, then free yourself from it by forgetting it! Then forgive him, which should be easy now that you are not carrying a list to remind you how he hurt you and then take the initiative to reach out to him!

You may say, well he's my father he should reach out to me. But maybe he doesn't know it's not too late. He may feel he's not worthy to have a relationship with you. He may think you are better off without him. But how will you know? We have to place it all in the hands of God and move forward! In the next chapter, we will deal with restoring a broken relationship with a son who is the blame.

There's one more thing we must do. You may have guessed it by now; you must repent! What? Yes, repent. Even God repented for making man and then repented from the decision to pay man for their sins. Thank God! But wait, you may ask why you should repent when you are not at fault. Remember God was not at fault but He repented. He wasn't guilty, but He paid the price as though He were. He repented for us because to him, having a real relationship with us was worth it. We were worth more than Him just being right.

A wise man once told me, "To maintain a healthy relationship with anybody you must give up the right to be right." So, in essence, God repented for being right. That's sounds crazy, but it worked. This doesn't mean you give up your right to self-worth or your human dignity or your right to be in a safe environment, emotionally, physically and mentally. If things are so severe, whereas you are not safe, seek help from a professional counselor or Clergy. I understand that those types of relationships definitely need mediation and intervention to become strengthened again.

So, God, we repent for holding back forgiveness, we repent for abstaining from reconciliation, we repent for being angry, being mad and for withholding love. We just decided that we will turn from anger to happiness, from unforgiveness to forgiveness and from hate to love. We take the power back from those with whom we are mad, from wanting them to give us a reason to be happy and decide we are going to do something about it ourselves in Your loving grace! We will be happy! Because we repented, we turn away from wrath in Jesus name

If your father is deceased and he died while you were still at odds try writing a letter of repentance and forgiveness to him. Express yourself fully and then visit his gravesite with it. If you can't visit his gravesite with it, write it anyway and put it in an envelope and place it in a safe place. Just getting it out and communicating it will do wonders.

There are some cases that the father is not ready to rekindle a relationship with you. That's on him. Don't take it personally. Everybody comes to their place of being in their own time. Your moves were to free and release yourself from the bondage of unforgiveness and anger and wrath. He will have to make moves to free himself as well. Don't return to the place of hurt and rejection. Instead turn to God, your heavenly father. He will always be there waiting for you with open arms.

Just note, that the issue from this point is not with you. It's with him. He may need more healing. He may need more time figuring things out. But you will have opened yourself to love and freed yourself from resentment. Never close that door and never enter into the captivity of hate again. Don't let anyone bring you there. Allow these scriptures to encourage you. Search your Bible for **Deuteronomy** *3:18*, **John** *14:15* and **Psalms** *27:10*.

As I conclude this chapter remember:
1. Forget! 2. Forgive! 3. Recall!
You will be glad you did!!!

Chapter Eleven

Stepping Back into Place: Part II

Re-establishing a relationship with your son

from a broken connection

Now it's time to talk about the father who is trying to establish a relationship with his child and go back to our examples in the previous chapter. Allow me to elaborate from *two perspectives*. First let's look at this from a viewpoint of the son being the one who broke the relationship:

"And he arose, and came to his father. But when he was yet a great way off, his father saw him, and had compassion, and ran, and fell on his neck, and kissed him. And the son said unto him, Father, I have sinned

against heaven, and in thy sight, and am no more worthy to be called thy son." Luke 15:20

I could not deal with reconciliation and fatherhood without mentioning this *verse*. In this text, we are looking at the third parable that Jesus gave, dealing with restoration and reconciliation. He dealt with lost sheep, then the lost coin and now the lost son.

We have suffered many losses, some economical, others spiritual and of course, relational. Whatever you have lost, the promise of God's word is that, if you put forth the effort, it can be found. With a sheep and coin, the onus is on the master/owner of those items to find it, because a lost coin and lost sheep can't find themselves. However, with a lost son, both he and the father had the responsibility to play a role in recovering their relationship. The son had to come to his senses. The father had to come to forgiveness.

The story lets us know that the father saw the son a-far-off! That implies he was waiting for him; he was anticipating his return. He was looking for him. One translation says he threw his arms around his neck and kissed him. The emotional driving force of the father was compassion; not anger or bitterness, nor resentment.

The son said I want everything that's coming to me, now! He wanted what he should have gotten from his father when the father died. So, in essence, he was really saying; Father, act as though you had died and given me my inheritance now. I will live as though you are dead.

Then the father gave him his inheritance; this is really what was passed down to the father, maintained by the father and of course added to by the father. However, the son spent it in a matter of days. He completely wasted his inheritance on undisciplined living. Wow! Can you imagine working your whole life for something and then someone comes and squanders it away in a matter of moments? What took a lifetime to amass was spent in days. The value or lack thereof here was in the life of the father's son. So instead of being angry, the father was moved by compassion.

Let's quickly look at another scripture and then I will share some practical tips for application:
"For this, my son was dead, and is alive again; he was lost and is found. And they began to be merry..." Luke 15:24

Powerful! The father understood that the son was dead figuratively, he was dead to his righteous ways and righteous teaching. Dead in a relationship... But now he's alive again. He was lost but now is found! The only mood to be in was a merry, happy celebratory mood. It was no time for anger or resentment. The father forgot the loss of all his valuables that the son misappropriated. He forgave the son and was waiting for his return with compassion.

To the fathers whose son has sinned against you, follow this example and be moved by compassion, not lost things. Forget so that you can forgive and recall. As we covered in the previous chapter.

Now the Son came not to be counted as a son, but as a servant, a slave. He did not feel worthy to be a son. The father initiated the reinstatement of his sonship. The father put that into motion. He was not trying to have his son stay dead in a relationship. He was waiting for the son to return so he could receive him again, not as a slave, but as his son! If the father hadn't forgiven him, he would have received the son as a slave; that is if he received him back at all.

When we don't forgive people, we count them as a slave attempting to make them pay off the debt of their offense. This is exactly how the son was re-approaching because he knew what he did to sin against his father. He didn't know that his father was looking for his return or that he was already forgiven.

If you are a father reading this right now, ask yourself, what are you looking for when your son returns? Are you looking for him to repent? Are you waiting for him to list what he was sorry about before you move forward? Hopefully, you are waiting to throw your arms around his neck, kiss him and restore him with the love of a father, therefore, giving life back to the relationship of fatherhood and sonship.

As I stated in the previous chapters, you can give up your right to be right and not be wrong. To restore the relationship, you must come out of your seat of right and meet him who did you wrong for restoration. Is not the relationship of your sons and daughters worth more than money, gold, pride or even hurt?

So, father, I beg you not to sit in the seat of judgment but run on the path of restoration and reconciliation. Let that child know that whatever they did, it was not great enough to match the value you have for them being in your life. Remember, forget the loss, so you can forgive the cost and recall the relationship back into its proper place. That's reconciliation at its best!

Now I will like to focus on Fathers restoring a relationship with a son, he has sinned against.

Piggy-backing on the above, son lets trade places with the father. In this case, let's put the father in the place of the son and vice versa. Now let's look at this from the view of the father as being the transgressor of the relationship. We remember from the story, the son came to his senses, acknowledged his faults and approached the father from a humble place. Likewise, the father who sinned against the relationship must do the same.

Fathers, you must come to your senses and acknowledge your sins against the relationship and decide to go back. When you go back, I advise you not to go back high and mighty. Don't return to the house saying things like, *"I'm in charge here, get out of my chair because I'm back. Go to bed at 9 pm. The father is back and it's time to get this house in order!"* No! You must earn the place of trust and power! Besides, depending on how long you were gone you may have missed those moments of child rearing; your child might be grown. Now that doesn't mean you are not needed or wanted. It just means you should readjust your provisions.

The top priority of your provisions is a true heart of repentance and humility. Come prepared to say sorry and own up to your faults against the relationship. Come back humbled, just desiring to serve, not proud and looking to *be* served.

Now a father's return to a son's life is a little different from a son's return to a fathers' life. They are in two different spaces of time. They are in two different places of maturity. The father has lived life and maybe at the twilight of his years. Therefore, his focus is on posterity and setting his house in order; making sure the family is secure especially considering his departure from this world.

The son is not always there. They may be focused on building wealth, establishing themselves in life and maybe, even living life unapologetically to the fullest. They may feel like they have time to get their house in order, but right now their focus is just building. They will require more time, more patience and more understanding.

Unlike the father, they need an explanation. If the father left while they were young, the question is: Who helped to shape their identity, their security and their moral structure? Who instilled the virtues and values in their heart? Who validated them? Who affirmed them? Who confirmed them? Why weren't you there? Where were you? Was I not good enough to be your son? So most often, before they can move forward they need to have an explanation of the past and know why this happened. They need to know it wasn't something they did that drove their dad away. They need to know what was so important, so valuable that exceeded the love and value of raising them.

Honestly, you may have the greatest reason, or you may not have a reasonable answer at all. The only thing that matters is that you give your truth. Try not to be a victim. Remember, you are our heroes and heroes save the victims. It's unfathomable for us to see our dads as victims even though we know everyone can be or has been a victim of uncontrollable circumstances. It's better just to accept responsibility and give your honest account of what you could have done better. This will help your son to move out of the hurt of his past without you, to a promising relationship with you in the now.

Notice in our scripture the son chooses to enter on the lowest level of relationship. His focus was just getting back home.

Tip 1: Fathers, your sons/daughters need you to come with a spirit of humility and determination for reconciliation. You may question, why do I need to be humble? Restoration for a child is different from that of the parent, whether that child is grown or young. In my opinion, the younger the child is at the time of restoration the easier it is for the parent. However, at any age the child will put the parent to some tests! Yes, tests! You need to be humbled to take them. I'm not suggesting it, but in most cases, it will happen so prepare and be humbled. We're rooting for you, dad!

Tip 2: Know that your sincerity will be tested. You will be tested on your desire to reconcile and by what you are willing to do to reconnect. You will be tested by resistance to see your perseverance. We need to know that you are here to stay. We need to know that you will do anything to get back into our lives for good and this time you won't leave us. So we may throw you a cold shoulder. We may act disinterested. We may even look like we don't want you, need you or love you. All of these are just tests of your resolve.

Tip 3: Please don't fail the test! Remember that the older they are upon your return- the harder the tests are! But once you've passed the test of our mind (really a defense mechanism, so we don't get hurt, disappointed or let down again) you're home safe. Our heart is and has already been desiring a reconnection. If it was left to our hearts, we would just receive you with no test. But the mind is strong and makes it hard for one to do what the heart wants without proof that it is safe to approach! So dads... You can do it, pass the test so your sons and daughters can move on to a bright future with you in their lives! Don't crack under pressure! Don't give up on the test! If you do, then the test was necessary, so we aren't hurt again. Beat the odds!

Tip 4: You must exercise patience. Start small and build trust to make it safe for them to love. Do this, and you are well on your way to your seat at the head of the table as the father in action over the life of your blessed children.

Both father and son, no matter what side you are on, remember the focus is on reconciliation not what you lost nor your pain. It's about reconnecting and forgetting, forgiving and recalling. Understand that God will help you get there a lot faster.

Where Is My Father?

Consider this last thought of this chapter: **Disconnected until we pay.** I remember my phone being disconnected for lack of payment. When I called the telephone company to reconnect, they told me I would have to pay my past due balance before they would restore my services. The problem was that; I didn't have the amount they were looking for right away. Therefore, I had to remain disconnected until I could pay. Fathers, sons, daughters or just brothers, when we don't forgive we are saying to our loved ones; you and I cannot connect. There cannot be restoration until you pay me what you owe me, whether it be an apology, or pain, or us wanting you to pay restitution.

Most often the offender cannot pay what we think they owe us. In return, we lose, because of the disconnection and lack of restoration. Why keep losing? Forgiving is saying you are excused from even saying sorry; I just want to restore our broken relationship. You may be sitting there saying you can't do it; you can't forgive them and/or you can't go back. But you can…You can do all things through Christ that strengthens you! Consider the tips I gave you, put them in place and move forward. Look to today and a greater tomorrow instead of the pain of yesterday.

{I wonder what Earnest is up to…. Let's find out}

A Young Man's Journey Towards A Positive Self-image

The Pages of My Life

Mister President

Even as a very young child. Wait, I love when I say things like, "when I was young," and then I watch the faces of everybody- their face and body language is questioning, "What do you mean, when you were young? You're still young." I tell them, "I was old when I was young."

When I was very young, I always wanted to be something great. I knew that I wanted to be a businessman. I wanted to be a president and CEO of something. I wanted to be a real estate broker. Well at around the age of seven years old, I pulled off my first big deal. I was able to convince my sisters that my room, which was a corner room, was better than theirs. I sold my room to them via even exchange. If you knew my sisters you would know, one, that this was no easy thing to do; two, they are very strong ladies with even stronger wills; three they get what they want- period! So I had to make them want my room. Well, I did! You may ask, why? I had my eye on the office space. Yes, they had a double closet. Yes, I could put my clothes on one side and have enough room to make an office on the other. I could care less about how big the room was, which it was.

My only focus for this place of real estate was its potential for office space value. Deal closed! I got it. I created my office. I got one of my mother's end tables because she had two, but didn't need both. Meanwhile, I had no desk; I needed a desk. I took a crate from downstairs. They came a dime a dozen. I grabbed a lamp, took a few pictures from a magazine and used a very small fish tank I had won. I was done, I had an office. I would go into that office and I just knew I was working! I was selling something or doing some big business! I was Mr. President.

My business grew so much that I needed to expand my office space. The space I had, was too small for my business needs. So, I went searching. Eureka! I found an awesome spot! We had two bathrooms in our project apartments but only used one. Well, my mind said we only needed one. I hired my cousins as movers and relocated my office to that bathroom. I had a formal door and I was set to take over the business world.

When we moved to Long Island, Yep I finally moved up in the world of offices. I took the screened in sunroom from our

A Young Man's Journey Towards A Positive Self-image

high ranch house and you guessed it; I made it my office, (I couldn't have been more than nine years old). Please don't ask me what I did. Well, I'll tell you what I told those who asked me then- I did business. I had a beautiful corner office with windows. It was great! The only thing was, I had to share it with the owner's dog; a German shepherd. Hey, it was his space. This wasn't an easy feat for me. Because I was terrified, terrified, terrified of dogs! If I wanted my office, I would have to face my fears and make this dog like me so that I could have it. Besides, this office came with a desk! A real desk! Come on Mr. President, you've got to do this; so I did. Before long, the dog and I were best friends and I hired him as my security. My sisters were very scared of dogs and had no aspiration of facing their fears. This meant I would be undistracted in my new office space doing "business."

    As I grew a little older and became a minister I always had this to fall back on, just in case "the Minister" didn't play very well in my regular world, no matter how hard I tried to make them. So I had another identity to co-exist in the world outside of my church world. I would still be preacher boy, church boy. But for those who just could not get with Minister Robinson, they could deal with Mr. President.

Where Is My Father?

It so happened that I found customers! I was actually doing some business. At twelve, I was able to barter my landscaping services for one of my neighbor's marketing and advertisement skills. He was a black man who had a beautiful house, wife and a computer! Yes, a Mac! He introduced me to what would be my first love, Technology. He made a flyer for Robinson's Landscaping. The rest of the kids were just asking to rake your leaves but I had a flyer and business cards! Yes, I was in big business.

I went through my community, passed out flyers and worked; giving the money freely, to my mother to help out. I loved the money, but I loved the flyers more. I hated landscaping! But it was my business, so I had to learn to like it. I would continue on this path until the Lord sent me a sign that landscaping wasn't for me. What did he say? How did he say it? Well I would go over a wasp nest in the ground with a lawn mower. I had wasps stinging me everywhere! They were coming out of my t-shirt, my socks and even my underwear! Sorry TMI, but true. That's when I went back to the drawing board; I needed a new business model.

We bounced around a lot as kids. It was hard for my mother to cover all the expenses for a house with five kids. But mommy did her best. When we moved to Church Street,

A Young Man's Journey Towards A Positive Self-image

(not kidding) this was the biggest house we ever had. With three floors, my mother put my little brother and me on the lower level. It had two rooms. I would need my real-estate skills once again to carve out office space. I convinced my brother, (well I told him because I was older), we would share one room. You guessed it, I made the other room my office! This time, I had an assistant. He and I both had a desk. Again, please don't ask me what we were doing. We were doing business. I trained my new assistant to greet my guests (of which I had none). I would teach my assistant how to answer the phone if anybody called, (nobody called). However, I had to fire him after he was speaking badly about my pastor. That would not work!

At fourteen, I dressed up in my best white suit with a red shirt and went to McDonalds to ask for a job. Of course, I got it. I think they were impressed with the fact that I came so dressed. Or maybe it was that I rode my bike so dressed. I don't know, but I got the job. I did well until the 2nd day when they asked me to clean the women's bathroom. I didn't know women could be so dirty! Jeeesh! I walked out of that bathroom and resigned from that position. God didn't want me cutting grass or cleaning up after dirty people.

Where Is My Father?

One of my church friends said they had the perfect job for me. I was sold when he said I would have my own business. You know I was in. I called the supervisor, got interviewed over the phone and I was hired. Yes, I got it! I worked for a youth program that got kids off the streets and sold candy. We went on fun free trips and activities that I normally could not afford. The whole idea was to keep kids out of trouble. It worked. I loved it and I went every day except Sunday of course. I started out there selling candy door to door, not knowing that about fifteen years later I would become president of the entire company.

As I got older, about eighteen years old, I would establish my first company- Heavenly Printing! I would hone my skills on the same computer that my first mentor had used to create design flyers and business cards. I went back to having an office. I took over my mother's den and made a beautiful office out of it. This time, I had visitors, clients and customers! I would go on to establish my second company Robinson Enterprises Incorporated (R.E.I.). Then I brought Heavenly Printing and PRO MAC (professional marketing, advertisement and consultations) under the one corporate umbellar, where they still exist today; the addition of two more sub-companies (house

A Young Man's Journey Towards A Positive Self-image

of Judah Daycare and Her Majesty, a clothing company my wife and I co-founded).

All of this was going on as I was growing as Minister Robinson. I was on my way to following my dreams of being a preacher and businessman. This time both worlds worked together and played nice. As Mr. Robinson, the president of Robinson Enterprises or as Minister Robinson, I was happy with who I was and how I looked. Earnest was still not allowed in my life.

Chapter Twelve

Father Figures

With a concentration on Spiritual Fathers

"For even if you had ten thousand others to teach you about Christ, you have only one spiritual father. For I became your father in Christ Jesus when I preached the Good News to you." 1 Corinthians 4:15 NIV"

Can one person change the world? Can one voice make a difference? I say absolutely yes! One of the greatest impacts anyone can make is serving as a father figure for a young man, young woman, boy or girl. I dare say, even for adults. They all need a father! You don't have to be a natural father to be a natural at fathering. By now you know how important it is for a person to have a father in their corner. Why not you?

You don't have to be perfect; you just have to be there. Share what you know by way of your life experiences, your successes, your failures, your setbacks and the comebacks. All your experiences have developed into what we call wisdom. You can save a life with the wisdom of your experiences. A father is concerned more about their children than himself as we observed in Chapter Eight -*Sacrifices of The Father.* **If you have a love for people and want to make a serious difference in the world, look for somebody to father.**

Let's explore some areas where your vocation can express a fatherly role:

Coaches can serve as *father figures*. The great coaches aren't just there for the win of the game. Instead, they are there to see their team win in life. Most often you'll find a coach refer to their teamsters as sons. He uses the venue of sports to teach teamwork, self-discipline, hard work and dedication. He's there to push them to win, but also to comfort them when they lose. Even in a loss, he turns it into a win by using the situation as a teaching moment and opportunity to build character, perseverance and determination. It could be said that the team plays for the coach. Remember, I shared the concept of the son earning the fathers praise. In this situation, the team could very well be working harder to earn the Coach's praise rather than the league's trophy.

Teachers can take on a fatherly role without crossing the lines. Teachers can stand proxy for a father by providing an image of a man of wisdom imparting knowledge. He would spend many hours with his students. As a teacher, you can make the decision to go the extra mile to show love, deep concern and create a bond that would last a lifetime in the hearts of the students. *Guidance Counselors* can do this as well.

The *Seasoned Worker*, is a person on the job who has both life and work experiences to share. They take young men under their wing and help them along.

My point is that, there are sons of all ages, just waiting for someone to come and father them, guide them and love them. Try it today, look for someone to bring under your wings and help them along in life. They may never call you father; but that's not the point. The mission of love and impartation is what's needed and most important!

Spiritual fathers

The most important *father figure*, with this title, is a *spiritual father*. I believe they play a very dynamic role in the lives of the children of God.

In our scripture reading for this chapter, *Paul the Apostle* is speaking to the Corinthian church, and implores them as his spiritual children. He points out that you can have many *mentors, instructors* and *guides* but have very few *spiritual fathers*. We also know that there is a difference between an *instructor/teacher* and a *father*. There is much to share on this topic.

I believe a **Pastor** is a type of a *fathering position* in the church. While we know that the **Heavenly Father** is the supreme source, the scriptures within the Bible are our greatest example of what a *spiritual father* looks like and how they serve.

For a brief moment, let's deal with an age-old debate on the use of the title **Father**. Some believe that it is not biblical to call men fathers based on what Jesus instructed in **Mathew** *23:8-12*. So let's look at it closer.

"But you, do not be called 'Rabbi'; for One is your Teacher, the Christ, and you are all brethren. <u>Do not call anyone on earth your father</u>; for One is your Father, He who is in heaven. And do not be called teachers; for One is your Teacher, the Christ. But he who is greatest among you shall be your servant. And whoever exalts himself will be humbled, and he who humbles himself will be exalted."

Doctrine (official teaching) cannot be established by one verse of text, but rather by contents of established truths of the scripture which correlates to contextual thought process. Basically, the official teaching of the church cannot be established based on one verse of scripture.

Therefore, we can't just take the line, "call no man father" and make a doctrine of the church with it. That is not to say, Jesus words needs a co-signer as if HIS word isn't enough for us to just simply obey. However, we want to make sure we properly understand, exactly what He is telling us, so we can obey without missing the point.

Keep in mind that the bible teaches us that the letter kills but it is the sprit that gives life. We must then understand the spirit of the text, the motivation of the text and the intent of the text so we can obey the text.

We must ask ourselves was Jesus forbidding us to refrain from referring to our biological dads' as father? Well, if we take this one verse literally, then the answer would be yes, we are not allowed to call our dads of any kind fathers. Be it father, God-father, Grand-Father Great Grand-Fathers. Because according to the text, we have one father which is God in heaven. And as such, even our fathers are really our brothers warranting no special honor.

Look at it, He did not in this verse distinguish between religious fathers, governmental fathers (Kings, lords, governors) and natural fathers (fathers, grandfathers), He just said, call no man on earth fathers, period. Once again, if we are to obey Him, we must understand Him. If we are to understand Him, we need Him to give us preachers and teachers that will rightly divide the word of truth, those teachers would need to study to show themselves to be approved to carry out such a task as encouraged by Paul the Apostle.

The conflict we are confronted with by taking Jesus' command at face value is it that, it encourages disobedience to one of the **10 commandments** *(to honor thy mother and father).* How can I honor my father, if I am not able to recognize him as father? It would also contradict Jesus reference to our earthen fathers, when he was expressing the supremacy of God's goodness over the goodness of our earthly fathers. *(Matthew 7:11)*

We must step back and comprehend the content of which Jesus is speaking, the background of which He is speaking from, and the audience He's speaking to. Then find its application to our lives.

After taking out time to study His whole discourse; we see that Jesus is really dealing with the **pride and arrogance** of the *Pharisees* and *Scribes* who He called Hippocrates and rebuked them for shutting up the kingdom of God from the people. (Making it very hard to live holy, because of the great religious demands that they put on the people.) He was attacking their prideful ways and how they required the people to bestow so much honor onto them. Jesus pointed the focus of the people to God The Father, as the source of *revelation, honor* and *commendation*.

He was also dealing with His disciples; He was breaking them from the system of this world (*gentiles*), power hungry and power seeking men who just want the respect of men and boast in their pompous ways. It's important to appreciate what it means to be a disciple. **Disciples** is a disciplined learner. Who takes on the school of thought of his teacher. They love learning from their master (teacher) and one of them usually becomes master/teacher themselves, replacing the original master, upon retirement or new assignment or even in some cases death.

One of the issues among the disciples was who would replace Jesus as the Master of the group, the head teacher, the one who's in charge (*Matthew 17, Mark 9, and Luke 9*). It was this seeking of position that Jesus wanted to dismantle from them and replace it with a heart of a servant. Thus, it was a double message.

> 1. To the general public of Israel that was under religious rule of the scribes and Pharisee as the official interpreters of the law, <u>not to call them "father", or "master"</u>; feeding into their ego, as they have not been authorize by God to reveal the mysteries of the word of God but commissioned by man to interpret the law, really placing them under religious chains.

> 2. To the disciples, it was a message for them not to follow the trend. Not to look for man to feed their *ego*, or to place them self in *positions of power* for the sake of their pride but for them to take on the heart of the servant. And serve one another.

As a bonus, it was also a message to the disciples that none of them will replace Jesus as the group's master, or head teacher, or father. He was extinguishing their fire for supremacy and letting them know they are all brothers to each other, co-laborers, co-servants working together with him and taking away the corporate ladder and replacing it with a humbled servant's heart.

Now Jesus says this in **Matthew 28:16-20**

"Then the eleven disciples went to Galilee, to the mountain where Jesus had told them to go. When they saw Him, they worshiped Him; but some doubted. Then Jesus came to them and said, "All authority in heaven and on earth has been given to me. Therefore, go and make <u>disciples</u> (student) of all nations, baptizing them in the name of the Father and of the Son and of the Holy Spirit, and <u>teaching (becoming a master, teacher)</u> them to obey everything I have commanded you.

And surely I am with you always, to the very end of the age."

Would not this contradict the above? Not at all! Christ authorizes the leaders he wants in his body. Servant leaders who have sat under his teaching are now leaders who are ready to go out and give out what was given to them instead of them <u>staying</u> in a circle among themselves and picking a leader to replace Jesus. John's disciples followed him until <u>he pointed them to Jesus!</u> Jesus says I'm not sending another leader to you guys; I'm sending the Holy Ghost who will lead you by the spirit. But you are to lead others to the same freedom and liberty that I have lead you. And make disciples in all the world. A disciple needs a teacher. Jesus says, the teachers will be those who were taught by Me.

"When they had finished eating, Jesus said to Simon Peter, "Simon son of John, do you love me more than these?" "Yes, Lord," he said, "You know that I love you." Jesus said, "Feed my lambs." Again Jesus said, "Simon son of John, do you love me?" He answered, "Yes, Lord, you know that I love you." Jesus said, "Take care of my sheep." The third time he said to him, "Simon son of John, do you love me?" Peter was hurt because Jesus asked him the third time, "Do you love me?" He said, "Lord, you know all things; you know that I love you." Jesus said, "Feed my sheep. John 21:15-17

Here we see not only Jesus reinstating Peter back into the fold after his denial of Christ. But we see Jesus charging Peter to feed the flock of God, who were, God's children. God the Father was setting up provisions of spiritual nutrients through Jesus, by his disciples.

Notice the two terms <u>sheep</u> and <u>lambs</u> were mentioned. Lambs, as we know, are sheep under one-years-old and sheep are adults. So Jesus was telling Peter, I have lambs coming that need nurturing and development; those lambs will turn into sheep that will need feeding and a shepherd. It was a commission to be a servant leader, but to continue to understand that they are His and not Peter's.

This point reaffirms the fact that the heavenly father is the supreme source. His servants carry out His will in the earth realm. Jesus was not talking against fatherhood; He was talking against the pride of religious leaders who just teach a law or tradition but are not fathers in the spirit, commissioned by The Father to carry out his will.

"Return, O faithless children [of the twelve tribes],' says the LORD, 'For I am a aster *and* husband to you, And I will take you one from a city and two from a family—And I will bring you to Zion.' "Then [in the final time] I will give you [spiritual] shepherds after my own heart, who will feed you with knowledge and understanding." Jeremiah 3:14-15

God wants to give us shepherds that will feed us, expressing the love of the Father who cares for His children.

Remember that our chapter theme scripture is another reference on spiritual fatherhood and pastors comes from the Apostle Paul in *1 Corinthians* 4:14-15.

"For though you have countless guides in Christ, you do not have many fathers. *For I became your father in Christ Jesus through the gospel."*

By referring to the Corinthians as his spiritual children, The Apostle, implies his roles as a spiritual father. The Apostles Peter, James and John do the same. Since the Bible frequently speaks of this spiritual fatherhood, we have established that we can acknowledge spiritual fathers without fear of disobeying Jesus. Our Lord acknowledges spiritual fathers in the faith, as long as they are God sent, with a God sent mission and we don't confuse them with God himself.

I have a little more information to share and will go into understanding the difference between natural and spiritual fathers and how we can work with them to accomplish the will of God for our lives.

There are, of course, some similarities, but the differences can cause one to feel disheartened because of failed expectations. The job description for a *spiritual father* and a *natural father* are somewhat different. There are many times that the pastor is looked to as the father, especially in the African American church.

According to many statistics, the fatherless homes within the *African American* community are the highest among other racial and *ethnic* groups. Because there is a void of a 'father' in the home, expectations can cause major setbacks and disappointments in one's *spiritual* walk. We already covered the job of a *natural father* but let's cross compare and look at the *spiritual father*.

SPIRITUAL FATHER	NATURAL FATHER
Well-Being	Well-Being
Spiritual Development	Spiritual Development
Teach Biblical Principles	Teach Biblical Principles
Discipline	Discipline
	Spend Quality Time
	The Main Provider of Basic Needs

As we can see from the list, in some areas both can provide the same things. However, the natural father has way more responsibility to fulfill. Those of us who run, live in or come from single parent households without a father must understand that the 'spiritual father' is not your father. There should not be an expectation for him to do more, especially if he has a family of his own. Note that natural and spiritual fathers can co-exist together in caring for the well-being of the son in the areas highlighted above.

I can be honest and share that growing up without a father actively in my daily life. I wanted my pastor to fill that void which created a silent tension in our relationship. He couldn't do what I would have liked because he was commissioned by God to father me spiritually.

I didn't fully understand it until I became a father and then became a pastor. Only then did I truly understand that I wasn't being rejected or disliked by my pastor; but in reality, I was expecting him to occupy a position that was beyond his holy calling. I have three kids and they require so much love, attention and support. I could not imagine having to play the same role for any more than maybe two more kids. Five is my limit. Does this mean I don't love my congregation or don't want to spend time with them? No, it's just an unrealistic expectation. Moses observed this and understood this all too well:

"Moses heard the people of every family wailing at the entrance to their tents. The LORD became exceedingly angry, and Moses was troubled. He asked the LORD, "Why have you brought this trouble on your servant? What have I done to displease you that you put the burden of all these people on me? Did I conceive all these people? Did I give them birth? Why do you tell me to carry them in my arms, as a nurse carries an infant, to the land you promised on oath to their ancestors? Where can I get meat for all these people? They keep wailing to me, 'Give us meat to eat!' I cannot carry all these people by myself; the burden is too heavy for me. If this is how you are going to treat me, please go ahead and kill me—if I have found favor in your eyes—and do not let me face my own ruin."

Numbers 11:10-15

Boy I bet most pastors have felt this way. Moses just didn't have a prophetic ministry, He had a pastoral ministry. He fathered the nation of Israel. He felt the weight of his assignment. He also had a princely charge because as a king cares and leads his people, through laws and justice, Moses had to do the same. He felt the pressure and it was overwhelming! It was so heavy that he asked God to kill him! Wow!

Some of you are just now getting a real glance into the plight of your spiritual leaders. From a distance, he looks glorious, but that's from your tent. But the burden is real! Let's look at another account of Moses entreating The Father for additional help as he cared for God's flock.

"Now Moses used to take a tent and pitch it outside the camp some distance away, calling it the "tent of meeting." Anyone inquiring of the LORD would go to the tent of meeting outside the camp. And whenever Moses went out to the tent, all the people rose and stood at the entrances to their tents, watching Moses until he entered the tent. As Moses went into the tent, the pillar of cloud would come down and stay at the entrance, while the LORD spoke with Moses. Whenever the people saw the pillar of cloud standing at the entrance to the tent, they all stood and worshiped, each at the entrance to their tent. The LORD would speak to Moses face to face, as one speaks to a friend. Then Moses would return to the camp, but his young aide Joshua son of Nun did not leave the tent. Moses said to the LORD, "You have been telling me, 'Lead these people,' but you have not let me know whom you will send with me. You have said, 'I know you by name and you have found favor with me.' If you are pleased with me, teach me your ways so I may know

you and continue to find favor with you. Remember that this nation is your people." Exodus 33 7-13

Look at this, Moses pitched a tent outside the camp. And from there he connected with God. When God's presence would descend into the tent to talk to Moses, the people would see the Glory and worship God at their tent. So from their tents, Moses looked powerful! Mightily! He who spoke to God, face to face, glorious even but from Moses tent, he was crying about how weak he really was, how much he needed God to assist him in this great task. The people saw one thing from their tents, but Moses knew another.

As it is written:
"For your sake we face death all day long;
We are considered as sheep to be slaughtered."
Romans 8:36

If you are a Pastor, I commend you for accepting the challenge as Moses did. Please remember that God will be with you. Moses understood that God had to go with him so he can draw from Him to meet the ever so pressing demands of the people. Moses did not try to take position or ownership of God's children. Instead, he served as a father expressing the love from The Heavenly Father. He had no problem reminding God that these were His children, His people and His mission.

Does that mean Moses' didn't want to serve as the pastor, prophet or prince, absolutely not; he was more focused on the reality that without God he cannot do anything. Spiritual Fathers have the awesome task of pointing the children of God to the Father, and teaching them the ways of God and leading them to the path of their God-given destiny.

As I end this chapter, I hope you have a clear understanding of the role of Spiritual Fathers. We will touch upon it a little more in the next chapter of *Spiritual Sons*.

Calling your attention back to the above text of scripture. Notice that everybody was at the entrance of their tent, didn't even stand in front of the tent of Meeting. However, Joshua did not leave his Spiritual Father's tent. Here we have it established that Nun was Joshua's paternal father, however we see him so connected to Moses that he didn't leave when the presence of God would come to deal with his spiritual father. I know previously I said the spiritual father doesn't' have the same amount of time as the paternal father and have different functions. That's still true. But in some cases of *spiritual sons* there is an exception. Everybody in your congregation is a child of

God (well pretty much everybody) and God requires the leader to express the fatherly love to them all. However, there is a hand selected few, the chosen out of the called that needs to be at hands-reached for more intimate fathering and developing.

Chapter Thirteen

Spiritual Sons

Jumping right in where we left off in *chapter twelve*. I want to focus on *spiritual sons*. Joshua was such a one. But in this case, he is not called Moses' Son; he is called Moses' Aid. In other words, his level of access to Moses is through *servitude*. See, in the kingdom *sonship* costs. The cost of sonship is servitude. Let's explore this thought process further:

Remember Jesus told his disciples the greatest among you is the *servant*. In the kingdom of God, *servants-sons* become *successors*. Even Our Lord and Savior was a servant son.

"Who, being in very nature God, did not consider equality with God something to be used to his advantage. Rather, he made himself nothing by taking the very nature of a servant and being made in human likeness. Being found in appearance as a man, he humbled himself by becoming obedient to death—Even death on a cross. Therefore, God exalted him to the highest place and gave him the name that is above every name, that at the name of Jesus every knee should bow, in heaven and on earth and under the earth, and every tongue acknowledge that Jesus Christ is Lord, to the glory of God the Father." (Philippians 2:6-1)

Jesus was a servant son. He didn't take on an elite mindset, or entitlement disposition, but he served the Father whole heartedly and humbly. He said I always do the things that please my father. He also said to his earthly mother Mary, I must be about my father's business.

These are a few qualities of good spiritual sons:
- A. Spiritual sons are not looking for public endorsement without private mentorship.
- B. Spiritual sons are not looking for an opportunity to shine as much as an opportunity to serve.
- C. Spiritual sons understand and the value training from their leader.
- D. Spiritual sons have the heart to lift their leader's burden.
- E. Spiritual sons know that the wisdom and knowledge cost their leader something great. So at the very least, their heart is to work off the school tuition.
- F. Spiritual sons want to serve because they believe in the leader's Godly calling and understand that helping the leader fulfill their vision is being a part of God's plan.

Four Spiritual Father/Son Relationships in the Bible.

Elijah and Elisha

When *Elijah* requested God to end his term of service, (and that's putting it lightly) God told him he had more work to do. One of the jobs was to raise up a successor, Elisha. The Lord God commanded that Elijah place his mantle on him. Now it was up to Elisha to take what he got and run with it, or trade it in for what could be behind "curtain number one." Many times, people approach a spiritual father like he's a magician; a quick trick, abracadabra and *"poof"* you're at your place of destiny. No. If God gives you a mantle, you must serve the previous owner of that mantle. Why? Not because you're paying for it, but because you are learning from it. Every task is a learning experience with hands on training!

Now *Elisha* could have gotten caught up with the crowd because Elijah had "sons of his office" who followed his office more than they followed him. They were trying to convince Elisha to stop following Elijah and follow them, because Elijah was being taken up any day now. Knowing that their father was soon to leave them, what did they do? Well, they did not make good use of the precious time they had remaining with their father, that's for sure. Why? It could very well be as I previously stated that they were "sons of the office." What's a "son of the office"? I'm glad you asked. A *son of the office* is someone who is loyal to your gift, but not to your mission, assignment or person. These are not fit to succeed you. These are opportunists who like the gift but don't care for the Giver or His mission. They tried to get Elisha to stop following because they knew that God was about to take Elijah home to glory. But Elisha was after something and he would not let Elijah out of his sight.

As a matter of fact, Elijah tested him and tried to get him to stay home and not go on some of the missions. Elisha passed with flying colors. Elijah asked his spiritual son what he wanted in return for his faithfulness and servitude. Elisha said I want a *double portion*! It's hard, but it's possible explained Elijah.

Check this out, when Elijah was taken up, his mantle fell! Elisha picked it up. He called for the God of His Spiritual Father! God showed up. But wait; there's more. When he went back, the sons of the prophet perceived that the spirit of Elijah rested on Elisha- his anointing, not just his *physical* mantle. They bowed. Wow! However, they were not convinced that Elijah was taken away for good. In times past, God would pick Elijah up in the spirit and carry him to his next destination (how about that for air travel, thousands of years before the first airplane?). They wanted to put out a search. At first Elisha said no, but then allowed them to do it anyway. They looked and came back with nothing. Elisha knew that God had carried his father back home to glory and he was left to carry on the work, the mission and the *charge*. The office stayed the same. However, the officer had been replaced. The sons of the office were loyal to the office; they were so far from him that they didn't realize he was gone from them. What was worse was that they didn't get all they could have, had they been a close son. Elisha joined their sonship last but came out first!

It's not about how long you've been with your spiritual father; it's what you get from him while you're with him that makes all the difference. It's important to understand that we don't know when the last time is the last time. With time being so unpredictable, let us make good use of the present to get and do all that we need to do while we have a chance. When you have time read the whole story told in *2 Kings, Chapter two*, to gain more clarity and insight.

Paul and Timothy

Timothy was a young lad whose mother was a believer and was taught about the things of God through his grandmother. His father was Greek. Paul meets him on one of his missionary journeys and the connection was made.

Paul poured himself into his spiritual son, not just from a general pastoral perspective but Timothy was "chosen" from the "called" to be raised up to succeed the Apostle Paul. He was not just there to service the apostolic office, but he had a Godly love for Paul and was faithful and true to him.

God would eventually use him as he was sent on assignments by Paul to strengthen the churches and be there to help convey Paul's heart to the saints when Paul had to rebuke them for their folly.

This is key as one of the most beautiful pictures of spiritual father/son relationship in the kingdom:

"But I trust in the Lord Jesus to send Timothy shortly unto you, that I also may be of good comfort when I know your state. For I have no man likeminded, who will naturally care for your state. For all seek their own, not the things which are Jesus Christ's. But ye know the proof of him, that, as a son with the father, he hath served with me in the gospel. Him, therefore, I hope to send presently, so soon as I shall see how it will go with me." Philippians 2:19-23

Timothy served so faithfully that Paul could not find anyone whom he could send who possessed that like-minded faith, as well as, the same heart and agenda as his 'spiritual father.' Not just for Paul, but Paul's work in the Lord. Again, this is what it's about; raising up sons who will not just serve you but will serve the mission, carry the mantle and operate in the *anointing*.

As Paul, the *Apostle* was fading off of the scene, he had confidence in his spiritual sons, particularly Timothy who would carry on the work in his absence. He also points out another important truth regarding sonship. Paul recognized that people are working in the kingdom but not for Christ. They are doing it for themselves and looking to see how they could benefit. As we stated before, when Paul had to rebuke the church for their folly and would send Timothy to deliver the message, Timothy would not give the message and use the visit as an opportunity to get ahead of Paul and steal the hearts of the people from him like Absalom did with David, but he conveyed the heart and love of Paul's mission to them. He was able to get them to see that Paul loved them and why he was so passionate about their *righteousness* and spiritual growth. He directed their hearts to their spiritual father. That's a son!

The Disciples

"Then the eleven disciples went away into Galilee, into a mountain where Jesus had appointed them. And when they saw him, they worshiped him: but some doubted. And Jesus came and spake unto them, saying, All power is given unto me in heaven

and on earth. Go ye therefore, and teach all nations, baptizing them in the name of the Father, and of the Son, and of the Holy Ghost: Teaching them to observe all things whatsoever I have commanded you: and, lo, I am with you alway, even unto the end of the world. Amen." Matthew 28:16-20

As you can tell, we are turning our attention back to Jesus and the *twelve*. They (the 12) started out as *disciples*. From discipleship, they were chosen to be His Apostles. At first, Jesus only gave them permission to go to the lost house of Israel, but in this scripture, He called them to the world.

From the time, He chose them to follow him to the time he appointed them, even to the time he commissioned them, he was raising them up!

He taught them like they were his kids and even said if you don't receive the kingdom like little children you won't get it. He broke down the kingdom of God unto them. He worked in *miracles, signs and wonders* and declared that they would to, if they believed.

"Believe Me that I am in the Father, and the Father is in Me; otherwise, believe because of the works themselves. "Truly, truly, I say to you, he who

believes in Me, the works that I do, he will do also; and greater works than these he will do; because I go to the Father. Whatever you ask in My name, that will I do, so that the Father may be glorified in the Son."
   John 14:11-14

In the interim, they served and worked as they learned. They helped Jesus to feed the hungry, prepare for his triumphant entry, prepare for the *Passover Supper* and many other things to learn and assist.

Remember Jesus just didn't pick anyone; he took time in prayer to select who would be his successors. He worked on their *heart,* their *soul,* their *spirits,* their *character* and their *integrity.* And of course, their *faith!* You can read more about their exploits with Christ in the four gospels *(Matthew, Mark, Luke, and John).*

<u>Closing out our storyline with Joshua and Moses</u>
   "...And Moses spake unto the LORD, saying, Let the LORD, the God of the spirits of all flesh, set a man over the congregation, which may go out before them, and which may go in before them, and which may lead them out, and which may bring them in; that the congregation of the LORD be not as sheep which have no shepherd. And the LORD said unto

Moses, Take thee Joshua the son of Nun, a man in whom is the spirit, and lay thine hand upon him; And set him before Eleazar, the priest, and before all the congregation; and give him a charge in their sight. And thou shalt put some of thine honor upon him, that all the congregation of the children of Israel may be obedient..." Numbers 27:12-23

One of the main tasks of spiritual fathers is to raise up spiritual sons to replace them. Remember a father is a seed bearing male. One of his universal callings is to be fruitful and multiply. He's to reproduce himself. **You're not a spiritual father if you are not looking to reproduce yourself.** This is not so you can reign over them but so that what you reproduce can replace you. **Can God trust you to raise up your replacement?** Joshua was with Moses all that time for training, not just to aid him. He wasn't just there to carry his "briefcase", but he was there to learn how to carry Moses' anointing. See, spiritual fathers must raise up the son to carry the mantle, the charge and the anointing so that the mantle, charge and anointing don't return to the earth with the father at his demise.

Today we have so many fathers who are dying with the mantle, the charge and with the anointing.

Look at our text. When God told Moses that his time was up, Moses asked God for his replacement. That's a father. A father doesn't have to be told to raise up a replacement. That was one of the first things he started doing. Most fathers want to have children when they're young. You don't want to wait till you're ninety years old to have children. Even Abraham wasn't happy about having to wait that long to have children. You want to have amble time to be able to raise them up correctly and effectually.

I am seeing so many leaders just realizing that their time on this side of the earth is about up, quickly looking around trying to find sons to father, so their succession is in place. Again, allow me to call your attention back to Moses when earlier in his ministry he had Joshua in the ten with him as he ministered unto THE Lord, now that same Joshua is called to replace him.

Leaders, you have to know when your time is winding down. We see now, how important it is to plant our successor in place through sonship. We must know when it's time to pass the torch. It breaks my heart to see how so many ministries are dying right along with the leader because he doesn't know when is when. If you are as close to God as you should be, God will tell you when it's time. Then you have to be strong enough to tell your son. Please, please don't wear the mantle into the grave.

Key points to remember:

True spiritual fathers are concerned about the care, wellbeing and development of their spiritual children.	Spiritual sons have a heart for their father.
True spiritual fathers want what's best for their spiritual children.	**Spiritual sons are like-minded with their father's faith and mission.**
True spiritual fathers look for a successor and begin to raise them up; enabling them to walk out and carry out the father's mantle with integrity.	Spiritual sons know how to honor their father's legacy by keeping the charge of their assignment.
Spiritual fathers know when it's their time to pass the baton.	**Spiritual sons are trustworthy.**
Spiritual fathers want their sons to exceed them.	Servant sons who have been called by God will succeed their fathers.

Chapter Fourteen

Don't be a Bastard

"But if ye be without chastisement, whereof all are partakers, then are ye bastards and not sons."
Hebrews 12:8

Jesus asked his disciples; Who do men say that I am? Then he asked the disciples, "who do you say that I am"? In other words, what are "they" saying about me? And does their view affect you see me? Peter declared that "Thou art the Christ, the Son of the living God!" Jesus replied, "My father had to tell you that!"

Spiritual fathers provide individualization and cultivation. A spiritual father gives honor. As with Moses, Paul and Jesus, they all gave honor and authority to their sons, so that their sons can be received by anyone who adheres to them or in the realm of their sphere of influence. As it was with God the Father and Jesus the Son; fathers must publicly affirm and validate the authority of their sons.

However, bastards have no such right. Understand that a bastard is an illegitimate son and he will not inherit the promise. Don't get me wrong, they are sons, just not legitimate sons. Bastards have no right to the inheritance because they have no legal claim to their fathers' blood, his name, nor his house. God did not call us to be bastards but he called us to Sonship. What's a spiritual bastard? In my view, it is:

1. Someone who cannot take a rebuke or correction.

2. Someone who refuses to be trained or developed.

3. Someone who will not submit to any authority or spiritual covering.

Now we're getting heavy. As I stated earlier a bastard is a son, yes, but he's a son with no rights. As a spiritual father, you may find that there are people who you gave birth to in the spirit but disconnect themselves from you afterward. They may preach like you. They may have your style. They may have your vocabulary… but they have no right to your mantel, because they are bastards.

Judas, one of the twelve became a bastard:

1. He wasn't happy about the rebuke of the Lord, commanding everyone to leave the woman with the alabaster box alone and allow her to worship from her heart.

2. He allowed offense to be the door the devil would use to gain access to his heart to betray Jesus.

3. He did not allow God the same access to his heart to root out bitterness and greed. Therefore, even though he was a disciple of Christ, a chosen apostle of Christ and a bishop of Christ he became a bastard; a son with no rights to salvation or succession. Wow! Instead, he became the son of perdition.

My friend, Don't let the devil harden your heart from your pastor especially in times of rebuke. That's the quickest way to give up your rights to sonship. The Bible says "whom the Son set free is free indeed". We have bastards in the pulpit preaching deliverance but have no right to free them that are bound. Why? Well, because they are not free themselves. They're not a legitimate son. They are a bastard so they don't have a right to the father's name, blood or authority.

They can speak it, but the father won't back it, because they disconnected themselves from the "father connection." The father connection is when God the Father, connects you to your earthly & Spiritual father and releases impartation, authority and spiritual legal rights to you. It's called Delegated Authority! You have power because the one who called you has power and gave you their power to operate on their behalf. When you disconnect from that power line, then you're disconnected from the source. So you sing, preach and pray, but there's no connection. You have positional authority, but no designated authority- which is delegated authority.

Jesus I know, Paul I know but who are you?

According to Acts 19, seven sons of Sceva, A Jewish Chief Priest was going around trying to cast devils out in the Name of Jesus who Paul preaches. They had the name right, but did not have the power source. They dropped Paul's name, even Jesus name but had no rights to the name. They were in a sense, Highborn, but that was of the natural course of nature. They were trying to use their positional authority that had no weight in the kingdom of darkness. This consequently rendered them exposed. Why, because they were not covered.

Honestly, going from a place of fatherlessness naturally, to being fathered spiritually can prove to be a great challenge. It's scary! It's almost abnormal for you! But it's necessary. You may have to get used to being fathered. That is corrected, rebuked, chastised, held accountable to, loved and cared for. You have to allow yourself to be free from your past voids so you can be free to enjoy the abundance of fatherhood.

Identifying your Spiritual Father and/or Son

Whoever you call your spiritual father could mean your success or failure in spiritual warfare. Last year as I was working on this book, I under a heavy spiritual attack. I began to pray. The Lord told me to call my spiritual father, Bishop Arthur Linder, Sr. and He instructed me to have him pray for me. I obeyed God. Even though I am a spiritual father. I needed my father to help get me through. I tell you I felt the breakthrough right away! God gave me the victory! We all need someone. It doesn't matter how high you sit or how modest your state is; we all need somebody higher than us to lead the way.

Spiritual fathers are not lords or kings but rather guides. A true father guides his children. He allows them to make mistakes and then helps them to learn from them. He allows them to make their decisions but helps to educate them, so they make wise choices. Your spiritual father doesn't have to be famous. After Paul's conversion, God blinded his eyes and sent him to a priest who was not very popular like the apostles, but his hands were used to release Paul's potential and recover his sight. **When you look for a spiritual father that is popular, wealthy or influential with the "in" crowd; you are not looking for a father, you are looking for a connection.** If so, you're playing a game of politics and can get very hurt. **True sons of the 'Kingdom' look for the heart, mission, spirit, integrity, authenticity and calling of God on the one they would call father.**

In most cases you don't find your spiritual father, your spiritual father finds you. In all of our biblical case studies, each son was chosen by God and revealed to their spiritual father. I think that's natural. I have never seen a son pick his biological father. That choice was not his. God made that choice on his behalf. I think the same is true for spiritual fathers. God made that choice for you. You just need to be open. **Don't allow a broken relationship with your natural father to hinder or distort your view of a spiritual father.** Let God do a new thing in your life and unlock your greatness.

We stated earlier that Jesus said, "greater things you shall do." Your spiritual father unlocks that greatness of God in you! He pulls your potential out of possibility into a now reality. Remember fathers are not mothers they are a little rougher, tougher and sometimes firmer, but that doesn't mean they don't love you. I believe mothers are there to heal your wounds and comfort you, whereas fathers are there to make you strong, so you have fewer wounds and ensure you're courageous and less insecure.

Also, in all of our biblical accounts each of the sons we looked at went further than their father. Some of you are calling your brothers fathers and wonder why you are confused. Brothers are in competition with each other. They want to outdo each other. **You are not a father if you are still trying to compete**

with your sons. You are still a brother. You are still on his level. You have not matured. Mature fathers do everything they can to make sure their son succeeds them!

King David was not permitted to build God a temple but did everything he could to prepare, his son King Solomon for it. Spiritual fathers, remember your job as a father is to train your replacement. Understand that it is an honor for your son to succeed you. King Saul did not have such honor. God ripped the kingdom from him. Now that did not mean God took him off his throne. That meant his bloodline would not carry the crown. His sons, grandson, great-grandchildren and so on would not be king and lead God's people.

God went completely out of Saul's bloodline, and even left his tribe of Benjamin, to step into the tribe of Judah, into the bloodline of Jessie and hired David. King David, the father, had the honor of knowing that when he died, his son King Solomon would succeed him. We can even track the earthly bloodline of Jesus our Lord to King David.

Fathers, how do you identify your spiritual sons?

"And the LORD said unto Samuel, "How long wilt thou mourn for Saul, seeing I have rejected him from reigning over Israel?" Fill thine horn with oil and go, I will send thee to Jesse the Bethlehemite: for I have provided me a king among his sons... And he sanctified Jesse and his sons and called them to the sacrifice. And it came to pass, when they were come, that he looked on Eliab, and said, Surely the LORD'S anointed *is* before him. But the LORD said unto Samuel, "Look not on his countenance, or on the height of his stature; because I have refused him: for *the LORD seeth* not as man seeth; for man looketh on the outward appearance, but the LORD looketh on the heart." Again, Jesse made seven of his sons to pass before Samuel. And Samuel said unto Jesse, "The LORD hath not chosen these. And Samuel said unto Jesse, Are here all *thy* children? And he said, "There remaineth yet the youngest, and, behold, he keepeth the sheep." And Samuel said unto Jesse, "Send and fetch him: for we will not sit down till he come hither." And he sent, and brought him in. Now he *was* ruddy, *and* withal of a beautiful countenance, and goodly to look to. Then Samuel took the horn of oil, and anointed him in the midst of his brethren: and the Spirit of the LORD came upon

David from that day forward. So Samuel rose up, and went to Ramah." 1 Samuel 16:1-13
(for the full text, please read the entire 16th chapter. Here, some portions are omitted for emphasis of our subject matter)

Here, God told Samuel the Prophet to anoint another King. This was in essence Samuels 2nd replacement because remember the Israelites did not want a prophet to lead them. They wanted a king like the rest of their neighbors. So God told Samuel to anoint Saul and he turned out to be as bad as God said he would be. Quick side note, did God make a mistake in choosing King Saul? No. God let them have what they picked so they could learn to rely on God's judgment and appreciate that He knows best.

Again, sons make sure you allow God to reveal to you who your Spiritual Father is and don't allow yourself to pick from the flesh. So now that Israel's ready for God's choice, The Father instructs Samuel to anoint another and get him ready to take Saul's place. Samuel goes to Jesse's house and sees some guys who he thinks might fit the bill. God says nope, that not what I'm looking for. Let's see if we can extract some points from this to help us look for our spiritual sons.

Where Is My Father?

God tells Samuel, stop looking at the flesh, who cares what he looks like on the outside? I'm concerned about how he looks on the inside.

1) Like Timothy, does he have a like-mindedness whose heart is after God?
2) Does he have a character of righteousness and integrity?
3) Does he have a meek temperament?
4) Is he open to correction, instruction, and development?
5) What's his work ethic?
6) Is he a lover of God?
7) Is he a worshipper?
8) What is his skill set?
9) This is very, very, very important: Will God's oil flow onto him?
10) Do you feel a connection when you pray for him?
11) Is there transference of God's spirit from you to him?
12) Will he receive from you?
13) Will the Lord reside in him?
14) Can he work together with the rest of your sons or daughters?
15) Is he open to change?

A Young Man's Journey Towards A Positive Self-image

Remember I told you we are servant sons, even though David was anointed king, his first step into royalty entailed being a worshipping servant son, and armor bearer to the king. Go back and read the rest of the sixteenth chapter of 1 Samuel. Look at what Saul's servant observed about David,

1. <u>Cunning (skilled)</u> player of the harp <u>(his instrument of choice indicates he was an intimate worshipper)</u>

One of the first requirements for spiritual sons is that they have to be spiritual. The second requirement is that he must be a worshiper of God because there is no way you can be spiritual and not be a worshipper; for the Father seeks worshippers who worship in spirit and in truth. Staying spiritual and having a true heart of worship is your biggest weapons against any obstacle. Don't be proud! God hates a proud look and proud people don't worship. They're too self-absorbed. They're too self-centered, and they're too busy soliciting worshippers to worship themselves. Saul made that mistake and the throne was snatched from him. However, if you remain a worshiper and spiritual, you will have no problems maintaining a proper spiritual father/son relationship. Not that you worship your father, but rather His God, which is the Lord God of All!

2. He was a son.

Son of Jesse- David was not just any son, but a servant son, remember we find him working when Samuel arrives to anoint the next king of Israel. He was a legitimate son, with the heart of a servant. He was not a bastard. Remember, our definition of a spiritual bastard. David was not like that; he was a son in good standing.

3. A mighty valiant man (brave, heroic, fearless, courageous,) in other words he was no punk!

He could hold his own. He would need this strength because to be a spiritual son of a king; you may be called to defend the crown. You may have to fight. People will try to convince you that what you are doing is not right. They may say to you that, "you are anointed to be king, not a slave." They may only see your works as work and not as a process; sometimes from good intentions or at other times from evil intentions. Regardless of their intent, you can't be afraid to stand up for the honor, integrity and righteousness of your assignment and your purpose in the life of your spiritual father. Not many will understand it, but you can't let them sway you like they attempted to sway Elisha from serving Elijah.

This level of valor, allowed David to have a true loyalty towards Saul. Now this never ceases to blow my mind! David was anointed to be the next king over Israel. God rejected Saul. However, David respected the fact that God anointed Saul to be King. He was loyal to Him even until his death. He was courageous enough to be loyal even though Saul eventually resented him simply because Saul identified God's fresh anointing on David's life and he was only operating under an old stale anointing, an anointing from yesterday. He did not feel God's empowering force today. As a matter of fact, he knew by this, God had rejected him and chosen another to lead his people. So what did he try to do? Kill David! Kill his armor bearer, his worship and praise leader, his minister who worked to serve him, who was only there because Saul himself asked David's father to allow him to come.

Even in all this, David remained faithful and true. Respected, honored, and remained loyal to Saul. That took courage, bravery and fearlessness! David had many chances to kill Saul but would not because he acknowledged the anointing that God put on him, even if it was an old anointing and even if God was replacing him. As long as Saul was alive, David honored the anointing on his life. Wow!

The point is spiritual fathers are not perfect human beings and they make mistakes. But God knew that before he called them. God made it clear through his word, rebuke not an elder, but entreat him as a father. Leave the business of correcting the spiritual father to the heavenly father who placed him there in the first place. Serve as a son! That's your job and your assignment. No matter what you see out of the flesh, remember he's God's anointed.

4. A man of war.

As stated previously, he would have to fight. This time, fight to defend the territory of the kingdom. If you are going to be a good father, you have to learn how to be a good fighter as a son. If David waited until the king was dead to fight and defend Israel, Israel would not exist by the time he would become king. You have to fight as though this is your baby because the truth is, it is. Whatever your Father has, is yours! It might not be yours now, but it will be inherited to you later. So fighting for it now will preserve it for you later. You may not get the stuff a natural son would, but like Elijah you get the mantle. Like Elisha, you have to fight to protect the anointing and mantle because when God takes your father up, that same mantle you fought for, will work for you. Fight now to protect the office you will occupy later.

5. Prudent in matters.

You can't be a spiritual son and be a dummy, plain and simple. You have to be sharp. You have to be wise, discreet and even judicial. Read! Read! Read! Study, as Paul told his spiritual son, study to show yourself approved that you may be a worker that needs not to be ashamed. The spiritual father can't give you brains and work your brains for you. You have a very important role in your development. David had all of these before he came to live and serve with King Saul.

6. Comely person

David was well groomed. Be mindful of how you present yourself. Remember you're serving under God's anointed. Comb your hair and brush your teeth. Bathe. Wash your clothes and iron them. Be neat and carry yourself like a nobleman. You don't have to be a self-observed jerk who's full of himself. But do look like you're walking with a king. Now it doesn't matter if you have one suit, one pair of shoes and two pairs of socks. Clean it, press it and shine it until God gives you more.

7. <u>The Lord was with him</u>.

Above all, this is the most important thing. Your spiritual father can't afford to carry sons of perdition with him. He's not Jesus. You must have the Lord with you. That is, you must have a relationship with God. You must know God for yourself. Your spiritual father is not your God. Some people think that if they walk with the pastor they don't have to fast, pray or develop a relationship with God for themselves. You better Know GOD FOR YOURSELF!

In short, 'The Lord' was with David endorsing his assignment and current path to destiny. God could be with us and yet against what we are doing. God was with Jonathan but was not for him being the next king. See Saul didn't have a problem understanding that someone would have to be king after him. He knew that he wasn't going to live forever. However, Saul wanted his natural son to be next. God chose another. God was not with Jonathan being king. But God would use Jonathan to help prepare the next king. Fathers, make sure God is with you on the choice of your succession. Remember, in all our biblical examples; God was the one who chose who will succeed their predecessor, not the other way around. After all, it's God's kingdom anyway.

Remember, not to follow the example of King Saul who competed with God for HIS glory. Or like Satan who wanted to exalt his throne over the throne of the Most High. Be grateful that God gave you a throne to sit on. Be like the Four and twenty elders in the book of Revelations who cast down their crowns and bowed their heads and worshipped the Lord.

Be like David, as we previously dealt with, He was a worshipper. When God told him he could not build a permanent house of worship for HIM, he was honored that God allowed his son to do it. Worshiping keeps you meek and humble, giving God thanks for even being chosen to serve.

So fathers, if we worship, it's hard for us to take on an entitled mindset. Only then will we be honored that God would allow us to start anything and our sons to finish what we started. Like Moses, Joshua would bring the people into the Promised Land. Don't allow the spirit of jealousy to consume you. That's one of the things that hurt Saul's and David's relationship. Saul heard the love and affection the people would give to David and became envious and jealous. You must be your son's biggest fan! You must be his biggest supporter! Because at the end of the day, he is you just in a different generation!

Spiritual Fathers, please remember it's all God's- His work, his church, his ministry, his chair, his time. Don't try to be God and select who's next, just execute your orders from Him. Carry out your charge. Saul chose Jonathan, but God chose David. God told Moses you won't lead them to the promised land but Joshua will! God told David, you won't build my temple but Solomon will! Be honored that God is still using your spiritual bloodline and didn't cut you out of the process. There are so many Saul's working under an outdated, expired anointing and wondering why the people are spiritually sick. Saul was so disconnected that he didn't realize he was replaced. Stay connected to God to know when your season has shifted. Know when it's time to stop climbing as a son and starting thinking like a father.

Spiritual Fathers, you can do well even when you messed up; if you own it. Use it to help your sons not to make the same mistakes. Don't be jealous, do better. **Leave a legacy of better**.

Let me close this chapter with this. God is looking for servant sons who are not looking for honor, glory or prestige but are searching for God, his will, his plan and his assignment! A servant son will eventually grow into a spiritual father. You don't have to be a senior pastor to carry out the task. Of course, you should be working in order and harmony with your local assembly. But a man of God may come in different forms- like a prophet, evangelist, king, priest, CEO, plumber or farmer. Whatever your calling, remember there is a son waiting to be fathered, nurtured, developed and processed.

Dear reader, now that we have a better understanding of the importance of our roles in the lives of our spiritual fathers and sons, let's make our heavenly father proud so that the Father may be glorified in the Son, by the way we serve each other as father and son in Him.

Chapter Fifteen

Our Father Which Art in Heaven

"A father to the fatherless, a defender of widows, is God in his holy dwelling."
Psalms 68:5

The night before I was rushed to the hospital for an emergency appendix removal, my appendix had ruptured inside of me. I was lying in my bed, sick and a little disappointed. I was disappointed because in times past, I would pray and God would answer. So I could not figure out why I was still sick. It was that evening as I was resting that I saw the Lord Jesus walk into my bedroom. He walked right through the door, while the door remained closed. He walked right up to me as I was sleeping and said, "fear not, let not your heart be troubled neither let it be afraid. For I am with you," then HE Placed his finger on the top of my lip and walked out and vanished this time instead of walking through the door. I was at the age of fourteen.

Recovering from surgery, I found out that my dad was coming to visit me. I hopped up to prepare for his visit. I went from room to room, looking for leftover balloons and chairs from people who had be discharged from the hospital. I wanted to make the room nice for my father, as I dragged myself and pulled my I/V bag on wheels to support my walk. Unfortunately, Dad got lost on the way and could not come.

Sitting there hurt and disappointed, I looked up to God and said, "Where is my father?" I had hit a breaking point and I wanted answers. I wanted to know who was supposed to teach me how to play catch. How would I learn to play baseball and basketball? Who was supposed to teach me how to talk to girls? Who was supposed to defend me against the bullies? Who was supposed to be there to make me feel safe? I cried and shouted to God, WHERE IS MY FATHER? His answer was simple; it was very clear and very strong. HE said, I AM YOUR FATHER! Wow! What a response! What an answer! God had taken ownership of me. That's the final message I want to leave with you. Ultimately GOD is our Father. I now know that is why Jesus touched my mouth. It wasn't to tell me to be quiet. It was for me to tell my truth, my story and my message.

Look at this:

> **"I will proclaim the LORD's decree: He said to me, "You are my son; today I have become your father." Psalms 2.7**

David said I will proclaim the Lord's decree! After this chapter, don't ask where your father is as though he doesn't exist. Be like David and proclaim what God has already decreed. Say what he said to you through his holy word! Which is, **He is our Heavenly Father and we are His children.**

Throughout the Old Testament, we get to know God as The Almighty, The I am, The Lord of Host, the Healer and the Deliverer. He is The God of Abraham, Isaac and Jacob (the forefathers of Israel). We see a God who requires justice and demands holiness. We see a God who executes judgment and shows Mercy. We see a God who creates and sustains. One who divinely chooses a people to call unto himself; people that will worship, serve and work for him. We see a God who is full of terror. As with the children of Israel the God that appeared as a dark cloud on the mountain, shaking the mountain and the people being full of fear, not desiring to see or hear God directly. Instead, they ask for God to speak through his prophet. We see humanity removed from the proximity of God. Far from where humanity started, where God would walk and talk with Adam and they could see him and interact with him face to face.

We have been so far removed that man wasn't even allowed in God's earthly house. Even his chosen people were not allowed to enter the tabernacle, only the priest and Levites. Still, only the high priest could come beyond the veil into the holy of holies. God was removed from among his people and from mankind. No father wants this!

A father is at his best when he can spend time enjoying his kids. Just recently my Father was ordained Elder in the Church of God in Christ and afterward, we went to dinner to celebrate. I watched him full of life and cheer as he sat at the head of the table and overlooked his children and grandchildren laughing, eating and enjoying the occasion. He was at peace. He was full of joy to see all his kids in one setting. At one point we were not all together, but God brought us all together again.

The same is so with God. Sin removed us from His fellowship and to keep us alive He had to remove Himself from us. Thank God who gives us the victory and causes us to triumph in HIM. At last, the family is brought back together again. But it was a lengthy process. From one perception, all we saw was an angry God not pleased with his creation.

Remember we even saw that God even repented of making man. Yet as with any father, He did not give up on us. He promised early in Genesis that he would send ultimate deliverance and salvation from the perils of man, and so He did. God sent and worked through Jesus His son, reconciling the world back to himself. It was like God was calling for a family reunion and re-gathering all his children to come back home and fellowship with him and each other again.

God used the Law of Moses to give him a legal right to deal with sin once and for all. This sin that has alienated us from our God made us strangers to our father and perverted his perfect creation. The Pharisees and Sadducees didn't understand that the law was only a shadow of what was to come. The plan of salvation was in Jesus. In other words, the Pharisees would not and could not see Jesus as the son of God. As a matter of fact, it was this that gave them what they needed to have him executed. See John 5:16-18.

They could not handle the fact that he was calling himself the Son of God. They knew what it implied. They were looking at it from a prideful place and a seat of entitlement. If they were the sons of God, they would enslave the entire world. That's because the Love of God was not in them as Jesus observed. The real sons of God also have his passion for his children and therefore their mission is to save and uplift, not kill and destroy. They were position hungry, because in their religious order, they were in charge. They were the big cats. Jesus didn't fit in their order, so they could not control him. What they could not control, they wanted to kill! Jesus was bringing another order and whole other system. They knew The God that demanded worship. Jesus knew the Father that wanted to show his love. See John 16:3

All they knew were rules and regulations, laws and traditions. On a side note they knew they could not fulfill but would use what they knew to rule God's people through condemnation. Jesus said, I have a better way, I have a greater goal and that is to introduce you to the Father and guess what I am the door to Him. See John 14:6. Jesus' goal on earth wasn't just to pay the cost of man's sin. His mission was to manifest the "THE Father" to us. Jesus has a mission of revelation. He is to reveal another dimension of The

God that Abraham, Isaac, Jacob and even Moses didn't see.

Let's look at his prayer:

> *I have <u>manifested thy name</u> unto the men which thou gavest me out of the world: thine they were, and thou gavest them me; and they have kept thy word. O <u>righteous Father</u>, the world hath not known thee: but I have known thee, and these have known that thou hast sent me. And I have declared unto them <u>thy name</u>, and will <u>declare it</u>: that the love wherewith thou hast loved me may be in them, and I in them.* John 17, 6, 25 & 26.

Here Jesus is telling God, that he manifested His name to the men that He gave him. However, the question remains; What is the name of God? What name did he reveal?

I submit, that the name that Jesus revealed to us was this: "**Father**". I am fully convinced that **Father** is His NAME! and to take it further, look at this:

> *"After this manner therefore pray ye: Our <u>Father</u> which art in heaven, <u>Hallowed be thy name</u>."*
> Matthew 6:9.

This is traditionally, known as "The Lord's Prayer". But some theologians would argue that John 17, is really "The Lord's Prayer". Because He's praying. So what do we make of Matthew 6:9? I dear say, it's The Lord's teaching on prayer, or how we should pray.

Jesus, starts His lesson out with directing us to whom we should address our prayers to. And that, my friend proves, that **Father** was not just His title, but Jesus was revealing to us a new view of the God we serve and we can call Him "Father" and that name is Hallowed (holy).

This had to make the religious leaders crazy. They were upset about Jesus calling their Holy God His father with all the implications associated. They must have had an absolute fit when he taught us to refer to God as Father. He did something powerful! He shared ownership of his father with us. In other words, he says, he's not just my father- But he's your father too. That's the glory, the honor that He shared. He had the glory and the honor of being the Son of God. That glory, honor and distinction gave He, to all of us! Glory to God in the Highest! He's our father too!

His mission was to reveal to mankind, that we had a heavenly parent, more than just God, more than just Lord Almighty! We can call him Father! Daddy! No one needed to go through a special messenger anymore to speak to his Father. Each of us had direct access through The Son. He put the religious folks out of a job. We could go boldly to the throne of grace, yes that mercy seat that's in the most holy place, where even the high priest could only go once a year; we can go beyond the veil and speak to our daddy any time we want.

"For all who are being led by the Spirit of God, these are sons of God. For you have not received a spirit of slavery leading to fear again, but you have received a spirit of adoption as sons by which we cry out, "Abba! Father!" The Spirit Himself testifies with our spirit that we are children of God..."

Romans 8:14-15.

We're not spiritual slaves that need laws and traditions to communicate with our father. We can call him by his new revealed name. ABBA! Father, that's daddy! It is a personal connection and an intimate calling for our father. This new name that Jesus reveals is not just Father, but Abba Father! His spirit cries out, revealing that name and bearing witness that we are His. We always were and always will be!

Jesus had a special mission to bring God's lost children back home to him. Not just his chosen people in the earth, (the Jews) but all people of the earth.

That's why we as preachers of the Glorious Gospel of Jesus Christ have been entrusted with the ministry of reconciliation. We are to tell everyone we know that God is our Father and has called us back unto himself. He settled the debt of our sin and brought us from the ownership of death and gave us the gift of life!

God says go ahead and ask me, call me, say, where is my father? I didn't know that God was my father! And He was there all the time. He promised never to leave me or forsake me. Natural fathers have their place, father figures have theirs, Spiritual Fathers are of high value but none can take the place or fill the void that only God our Heavenly Father, our Abba Father, can and will fill if we let Him.

When I came to understand this, I walked in a healing and restoration like no other. God accepted me just as I was, with all my mistakes, my issues and my pains. He fathered me and nursed me back to health and spiritual maturity. He used my both my natural father and spiritual fathers. But that day I heard him say, "I am your Father!" Go ahead and proclaim it. Go ahead and say it. God is my father! You are not alone. You are not abandoned and you are not rejected. It changed my life forever. I'm still finding out what it meant. God is, has always been and will always be there for you and me!

So why, why wasn't my father there for me? Let me answer from this perspective. In some cases it's not up to your natural father or even spiritual father to accomplish what God will do for and through you, so HE may allow them to go off the scene so that you can only see HIM. When you see HIM, it will all come together, make sense and fall into place- every tear, every wound and every let down will suddenly make sense.

Jesus says I came in the name of my father! Period. So whomever doesn't receive me, accept me or promote me, it's ok. Why? Because my father does. Jesus did not need the testimony of man, he had the testimony of the father. He did not need the witness of the court for he had the witness of the Father! The Father gave Him His name.

"Therefore God also has highly exalted him, and given him a name which is above every name: That at the name of Jesus every knee should bow, of things in heaven, and things in earth, and things under the earth; And that every tongue should

confess that Jesus Christ is Lord, to the glory of God the Father." Philippians 2: 9-11

Remember a father looks to push his son! Look at God the Father pushing His Son. We are a part of the body of that Son, even Jesus the Christ of God. So we are up there with him!

Now before I close, consider this. For most of my life, I searched for approval, validation and affirmation from man. When God revealed this to me, I realized that only what you do for Christ will last, and so what if nobody notices or praises you. He does, and that's all that matters.

Look at what Jesus says:

How can you believe, who receive honor one of another, and seek not the honor that comes from God only? If you really believe that Christ was sent to reconnect you to the father. And you receive that connection, you should as a son seek to please the father and have the father be proud of you and your growth. John 5:44

I leave you with this thought. God desires fellowship not just traditional worship as of lambs and oxen. He wants our heart. He wants us to dwell in his presence. The Bible speaks of a generation that will seek His face. Is this the generation that will seek the Father? The Father's will? The Father's word? The Father's pleasure and not their own? So many preachers are saying, well God wants to give you this and give you that and we start seeking God for stuff. But God told Abraham, that I am thy reward!

When God told me that He was my father, that was my reward. Sadly, it took twenty years for me to understand it and appreciate it. He alone is worth more than everything in my life. Our heavenly Father desires heartfelt relationship, not cold starchy worship.

I have three beautiful children and really what sends me up to a happy place is looking at how much they desire my attention, my love and my affection. It makes me feel wanted, needed and loved. God wants us to want His attention, His affection, His advice and His love. Seek the Lord while he may be found, call upon him while he is near.

Now I know what Jesus meant, when he said if we don't receive the kingdom like children, we cannot get in because God wants to father us! It is through the image of natural fathers and spiritual fathers that we understand in a tangible way who God the Father is to us. Once we get to know him as such, we will seek to please Him. Holiness and righteousness are no longer a list of rules, but a joy because it gives us access to His presence. Prayer is not a religious act or chore; it is an opportunity to talk to our Daddy and spend time with our Father.

Isn't that awesome? It doesn't matter how old you are or where you come from, we have a Father who's been watching over us all this time, just wanting us to get to know Him and see Him for who he really is- which is more than a God, but a loving Father!

Reader, take the time to seek Him, I promise He will be found of you and He is a rewarder of them that diligently seek Him. How can you seek Him, who you know not of? You know of God the creator, but did you know of God the Father who desires a relationship with you? Now you know! You don't have to go crazy trying to find Him because He's everywhere! Just stop where you are and call upon him. Say, Father I need you!

{Hopefully, Earnest made it to his desired destination. Let's see how he made out.}

The Pages of My Life

Earnest must live: I shall live and not die

> *for this son of mine was dead and has come to life again; he was lost and has been found.'*
> *And they began to celebrate.*
> Luke 15:24

I will make your name great! I was on a path to greatness. However, my motivation was off, my inspiration was flawed and because of it, I wasn't able to enjoy most of the milestones of success in my life. I always wanted more, was getting more, but even then was not feeling fulfilled with what I got. I was moving but never arriving at the place of gratification or satisfaction. At first, I just thought it was because I was driven and full of passion. The sad reality was that something was missing. I still hated myself. I was still looking for acceptance, validation and affirmation. I was unsure and felt unsafe. It didn't matter how many victories I won or obstacles I overcame. It didn't matter how many people applauded or cheered! I was missing something. I was missing the poked out chest of my father looking with a great sense of pride for what his son has accomplished.

A Young Man's Journey Towards A Positive Self-image

Being that my father wasn't there at first, I did everything I could do to please my "spiritual fathers". I walked around feeling rejected and unloved because I was looking for the wrong acceptance. It almost destroyed my faith in the church and even scarier; it almost destroyed my faith in God. Let's go back, just a little.

Everything was going as good as it could get it until I met my wife. I still remember the day. Of course, it was in church, for our churches fellowshipped with each other. I loved it because we got a chance to meet and see each other. Well, one day I mustered up enough nerve to speak to her. Wow! She spoke back! What made me sure that she was the one is that when she asked me how I made myself so available and valuable to ministry I explained I was the executive secretary to my bishop and learned so was she to her pastor. Well, that took me in. I said to myself, she loves my world, she is in my world and wants to do better in my world- my church world! However, still being self-condemning and not having a positive self-image of myself at all, I was very apprehensive to take it further. My "spiritual father" prompted me to move a little further and see what could become it. Well! Well! Well! This was not just a chance to find my true love but it was also a chance to make my "spiritual father" proud. That motivated me as it had in other areas of my life. I had to make a move. I had to show daddy I could get a wife. So I did. The only problem was Elder E. Edward Robinson II was not a human. He was an office. I dated and dealt with my wife-to-be from my strong suit. Oh no! Earnest could not mess this up. Besides, I was not just a minister anymore. I was an Elder; more impressive. So elder was dating Sister Clark. Until she asked me not to call her Sister Clark but rather me to call her Ebony. You probably figured it out. She wanted, somewhat, demanded to call me EARNEST! At this point, I was head over heels for her and she could call me anything her heart desired. She was my first real relationship and true love. What she didn't know was that every time she called my name Earnest, I would scream inside. I hated that name! I hated that person! I would go from screaming inside to crying inside. Every time she said, Earnest, it reminded me of everything. All the hurt, pain, rejection, mocking, molestation and rape that was hidden and buried had to stay dead. Earnest was a special education faggot. If I was going to make her my wife, I had to suppress Earnest until he did not see the light of day.

That created another problem. She would complain that I never took my "church hat off." I didn't understand what she was saying because again, I didn't know that Earnest was dead. I thought I was fine and she was just too worldly (supposed to be in the church but is secular). I had to bring her into spirituality. I thought I was spiritual. I was embodying a position. I created a world in the church and my position was my personality. Everybody that dealt with me, had to deal with the person I created. You dealt with Minster/Elder/Pastor/Rev/Prophet because he was and Earnest was not. To me, Earnest did not exist.

My poor wife had to weave through all of that and find Earnest! Because Jesus said it best.

"For when they rise from the dead, they neither marry nor are given in marriage, but are like angels in heaven." Mark 12:25

I had already died, gone to Heaven and picked up my wings. The human side of me didn't exist. Yet my wife was in love with Earnest; not the position I held in a church or the business world. This caused great conflict in my relationship with her. To be honest, I thought at one point she was the devil because she was trying to take me from the church but, in reality, she was trying to minister life to me! Jesus said I come that you might have life and that more abundantly.

Earnest was the man; the position was the office where the man would work. I had hidden behind my work so that Earnest would not mess up my life. Now if Earnest did not rise, my marriage would fail. Oh, I didn't tell you... Yes, we got married two years after we met! The Lord blessed us with three beautiful children. I'll tell you more about the children later in this chapter.

It still didn't hit me until I was preparing to be consecrated into the office of Bishop. Through the process of Episcopal consecration, everything in my life had to be settled and in place, mainly my family life and especially my marriage. Through the five-year preparation for the office of Bishop, we were mandated to have couple's therapy. We needed it because my marriage was on the rocks. It seemed as I grew in church my relationship at home would suffer. I was home, but not home, because my body was in the house but the pastor was in the home. My wife needed a person a human.

A Young Man's Journey Towards A Positive Self-image

She began to get hopeless and lose faith in Earnest, just as I had lost faith in him so long ago.

This process of preparation to episcopacy would reveal it all because all hell broke loose! My entire world that I created in the church was coming down like a meteor had hit and all life on my planet would cease. I was hurt because now I had no hope at all. My trust in God was for Rev. Robinson and this world that he created in The Church. For surely, the church is a safe place to build a world. Jesus promises that gates of hell would not prevail against it. It was the church that had that promise, not the world I created in the church. The gates of hell were taking no prisoners. Those who I thought were in my corner would be the very ones used to try to destroy me. After creating the world in the church and after creating a new man (E. Edward Robinson, II opposed to Earnest E. Robinson, Jr.) for the purpose of having a clean record with no name calling, no disrespect and no mocking; now, E. Edward Robinson, II was under heavy attack! I mean heavy. Everything I built on him was falling and being stripped from him.

I was at the greatest step of walking into the highest office in the church, but everything was falling apart. My church was falling apart with lies, scandal, character assassination and the works! Once again I was at a place where I looked and could not find my father. No one was there to fight for me. Nobody was there to defend me. E. Edward Robinson had failed me! The church had failed me! God had failed me!

At the lowest point in my life, right when I was about to give up and walk away from everything, God the Father began to speak to me. He led me to revisit Abraham's calling:

> **"Now the LORD said to Abram, "Go forth from your country, and from your relatives and from your father's house to the land which I will show you; And I will make you a great nation, And I will bless you, and make your name great, and so you shall be a blessing;" Genesis 12:1-2**

The father asked me what I saw. Of course, I mentioned everything but what he wanted me to see. He instructed me to look again. Then I saw it, "I will make your name great"- not your position, not your title. He began to let me know that all this time I was not working for His glory and that he used me for his purpose, but he wasn't getting glory out of my life.

A Young Man's Journey Towards A Positive Self-image

Full of tears,

I said, "Lord I started working for you over 20 years ago and you mean to tell me you weren't getting glory out of my life?"

He said, "I got glory from your works, and people have been blessed, lives were changed, but glory came from your works, not your heart; it wasn't in your heart to give me glory."

And I asked, "Father how does my heart give you glory?"

He said, "When I am all you are looking for. When my approval is the only approval you seek! When your heart to please me is greater than your heart to please your "fathers'"

I said, "Fathers... where?"

He took me down the path- your spiritual fathers in the church, your natural father at home and your business father at work. Any man that was above me who was established and successful and took the time to train me, help me and show me, I made my father. I made them the focus of my attention and wanted to prove to them I was worthy of their fatherhood. When they could not be there to celebrate my victories in business, at home or in church, I felt as though nothing mattered. So He was right, I was not working for God, I was working for me and my pay was my father's affirmation, validation and commendation.

Then what the old church mothers said came to mind; only what you do for Christ shall last. I did good things but it wasn't lasting because I wasn't doing it for God. God graced me because I worked hard; I put my heart and soul in everything I did. But my motivation was off and inspiration was off. It wasn't rooted in God. Even my family was for God, not me. It was for my fathers to see that I was a good husband/father. After taking a step back, I came back to God and repented for putting man in the place of where God the Father should have been.

Then I went to all my fathers and asked them to forgive me for resenting them for what they could not give me, because they didn't have it. They gave me what they could. They give me what they had. But only God could had to give me what was lacking.

As I turned the focus of my faith and works back to God, he made me realize that a son doesn't have to do anything to be a son. All he had to do was be born and stay alive. As

A Young Man's Journey Towards A Positive Self-image

long as he was born and as long as he was alive, he was son. Remember, God the Father was pleased with Jesus before he healed anybody on record or cast out any demons, remember, God said this is my beloved son, in whom I am well pleased. It clicked, the more I allowed God to bring Earnest back to life, the more I became human. I could open myself to love and be loved.

I love all my kids, each of them. As I was coming to the end of this book, my youngest daughter Nadiyah Grace Robinson was born. I was able to show her a type of love that I couldn't do for the other two. As I look at her, when her eyes light up and I see that huge smile, my heart melts and I say to my wife how I love that girl. The difference is that I now have begun to love myself with a Godly love. As I saw her, I saw me. Her sweet face of innocence moves me to tears. She didn't do anything, she didn't invent the cure for cancer and she didn't save the world from UFO's. I loved her and love her simply because she is my daughter.

God loves me simply because he's my heavenly father and I am his son. I didn't have to be a preacher for him to love me; I didn't have to be a bishop to make him love me more. He loved me because He is my Father! He wanted me to bask in his love, once basking in his love I can love and open myself to love others. He even saved me because he loved me! I didn't even save myself. He did because he's my father and because I am his son. "For by grace you have been saved through faith; and that not of yourselves, it is the gift of God; not as a result of works, so that no one may boast." Ephesians 2:8-9

God had to really get this through to me. He said to me, I can't make you great because you don't exist. That's when he revealed to me that I had killed Earnest. He revealed to me that's why I had so many problems in my relationships- because I didn't exist. I was not a human; I was an institution. God had to breathe love back into my heart so he could breathe life back into my body. Earnest must rise.

I felt like Lazarus who was dead, wrapped in dead clothes, dead beyond anybody's ability to bring back to life (the Jews believed that a spirit can come back to life within 3 days after death. But after dead, it was a wrap.) I was dead for so long, I wondered how I could live again. I wasn't dead in sin; I

A Young Man's Journey Towards A Positive Self-image

was dead in shame. God wiped my shame away and turned my pain into passion to help others.

Now I had a new problem. Earnest was dead for so long; I didn't know who be to the many who knew me as Edward or Bishop. When I would give a name without a title I gave my middle name Edward. But now I didn't have to use a title. Ebony and I were at a restaurant and we met a lovely couple who asked for our names. I began to introduce myself saying, "I am Earnest and this is my wife Ebony, we are the Robinsons." In the car my wife said she couldn't believe I did that! I said, "Me either, it doesn't hurt no more."

God kept his word and he made my name great. I am Earnest Edward Robinson the II. I am somebody, not because of my accomplishments, not because of my works but because God made me with his own hands, as he made you too! I looked good too. "For the LORD takes pleasure in His people; He will beautify the afflicted ones with salvation." Psalms 149.3-4

I hated everything about Earnest, even the way he looked. Today, because of God I have found peace within me. And I love me. And because I love me I can love you! "The second is like it, 'YOU SHALL LOVE YOUR NEIGHBOR AS YOURSELF.'" Matthew 22:39

You can't love your neighbor if you don't love yourself. God gave me the strength to love me in spite of my flaws and blemishes and what was done to me. Earnest is living! Ebony has a human being for a husband, not a church robot. The kids have a father, not an institution. My friends have someone they can cut up with and laugh. I threw down the grave clothes that I hid under. Just as Jesus called Lazarus from the dead, he called Earnest from the dead and he called me like he did Lazarus- by name! Jesus commanded them to roll the stone away from the opening of the grave and when he hopped out, Jesus commanded them to release him from his grave clothes.

Today dear reader, God wants to lose you from your grave clothes- you don't need them! You don't need the façade. God loves you just as you are for who you are. He will make you everything he intended for you to be!

I live free today. I'm still learning, because technically I'm only thirteen years old. As I'm closing this book, I am 1 year removed from when God brought me back to life. For over

A Young Man's Journey Towards A Positive Self-image

twenty years I had been dead. God was waiting for me to come to my senses like the prodigal father was waiting for his son, and just like God is waiting for you!

I am ok with being me! That's life. That's power! I am what I am and who I am is by the grace of God. God saved the last step of church hierarchy of leadership, the Bishopric to turn my world upside down and bring Earnest to life, so he can finally get the glory out of my life. Now from a healed place I have one of the most amazing relationships with my natural father. He is a great man of God with a mighty testimony. We talk at least once a week. His past was necessary for both his success and ours as his kids. For me to receive him, I had to let go of the past and live in today. That is something that he taught me and I thank God I have him in my life.

At the last hour, God reunited me with family I never knew. My Great-grandfather, Arthur Branch Sr. was one of the Founding Bishops of the Glorious Churches of God and died as the Presiding Bishop. My Grandfather was Bishop Arthur Branch, Jr. who was supposed to be next in line for the episcopacy but the Lord saw fit to take him home. So the mantle fell on my great uncle, Bishop Arthur Linder, Sr. who is the current serving Presiding Bishop. God busted up all our plans for my consecration only to send my great uncle, my apostolic father, to lay his hands on me and make me Bishop in the Lord's church. This is significant because it connected me to my forefather's mantle and Godly bloodline.

As he would tell me stories about my granddad and great granddad, that in itself brought such a healing. As he poured into me, I realized what a spiritual father is supposed to be. That has caused me to be a better leader to those whom God has placed in my care. What I thought was the end was only the beginning. Look at how God did this. He connected both worlds- the natural world and my spiritual church world, through fathers both spiritual and natural. What a mighty God we serve.

So no, I could not go back in time and erase my pain, but I can use it to help somebody. I also realized that as I father all my children, both spiritual and natural, there's a healing taking place. It happens every time I tell my son that I love him and am so proud of him just for him being him, every time I tell my daughters how beautiful they are and how loved they are, every time I pour into my spiritual sons and

A Young Man's Journey Towards A Positive Self-image

daughters and see them grow in God and in the grace and knowledge of the Lord Jesus Christ. It's almost like me inside them receiving all of this fatherly love.

You can help heal yourself by helping to heal others. Being a great father to your children, will help you heal from not having a father or a not so great one. I've realized that my pain turned into my passion and my lack turned into my mission to make sure no one feels like I felt. Now I'm more effective because, I'm healing from a whole place. I'm preaching from a healed place. I'm not doing it to prove I can, or that I am. But because of whose I am, who I have become and will continue to be.

As this book comes to an end, it's your beginning. Remember, God is our heavenly father from who all fathers receive their ministration. Each father in whatever category is supposed to reveal a dimension of the person and image of God the father, simply by loving their children and teaching them the ways of the Lord and life. As Jesus did, we will be able to show the world the Father, because Jesus is in us and they are in us.

Where Is My Father?

Let's show the love of the father and reveal him to everyone we know! For God loves you just for who you are. When I came across the true love of the father it forced me to love myself.

So now I have finally arrived. I have come to a place of a positive self-image not because I am perfect or flawless, but because I am loved with an everlasting love!

Thank you, Ebony, for never calling me Edward! You saw Earnest way in the back behind all the other stuff of which you were never impressed. You saw the best in me. God used you to keep tugging until Earnest surfaced, bruised, broken and hurt. I mean you even hated when your mother and family would call me by my title. Now I know what you were saying was that you were not giving up on Earnest even when it got hopeless.

Lord, I thank you for covering me until you changed me! Thank you for not giving up on me. Thanks to you the reader of this book for taking this journey with me. Now begin yours towards a positive self-image!

A Young Man's Journey Towards A Positive Self-image

Now that we know we are all Gods' children, will the real child of God please stand up? (Look out for my next book) a little harmless plug.

Appendix

FATHER STATS

There is a wide range of research and statistics related to the effect that fathers can have on their children. These statistics give an overview of some of the statistics about fathers and father involvement that is available. Additional research and reports, including the December 2013 National Health Statistics Report "Fathers' Involvement With Their Children: United States, 2006-2010," can be found in the NRFC Library. (www.fatherhood.gov/library)

70.1 million: Estimated number of fathers across the nation.
24.7 million: Number of fathers who were part of married-couple families with children younger than 18 in 2013

- 21 percent were raising three or more children younger than 18 (among married-couple family households only).
- 3 percent lived in someone else's home.

2.0 million: Number of single fathers in 2013; 17 percent of custodial single parents were men.

- 9 percent were raising three or more children younger than 18.

- About 44 percent were divorced, 33 percent were never married, 19 percent were separated, and 4.2 percent were widowed.
- 39 percent had an annual family income of $50,000 or more.

214,000: Estimated number of stay-at-home dads in 2013. These married fathers with children younger than 15 have remained out of the labor force for at least one year primarily so they can care for the family while their wives work outside the home. These fathers cared for about 434,000 children.

18% - In spring 2011, the percentage of preschoolers regularly cared for by their father during their mother's working hours.

Father Involvement and Education

When fathers are involved in the lives of their children, especially their education, their children learn more, perform better in school, and exhibit healthier behavior. Even when fathers do not share a home with their children, their active involvement can have a lasting and positive impact. There are countless ways to be involved in your child's education at all ages.

Where Is My Father?

According to a 2007 National Center for Education Statistics Report:

- 92% of students in grades K though 12 had parents who reported receiving any information from the school on the student's performance.
- 83% had parents who received any information about how to help with homework.
- 59% of students in grades K through 12 had parents who were "very satisfied" with their child's school; 55% had parents who were very satisfied with the school's parent-staff interactions.

The presence of a responsible father promotes improves academic performance and reduces disciplinary problems among children.

Preschoolers with actively involved fathers have stronger verbal skills.
Radin, N., 1982, "Primary Caregiving and Role-Sharing Fathers," in Non- Traditional Families: Parenting and Child Development, edited by M. Lamb, Hillsdale, NJ: Erlbaum, pp. 173–204.

Children with actively involved fathers display less behavior problems in school.
Amato, P.R., and Rivera, F., 1999, "Paternal Involvement and Children's Behavior Problems," Journal of Marriage and the Family, 61, 375–384.

Girls with strong relationships with their fathers do better in mathematics.

Radin, N., and Russell, G., 1983, "Increased Father Participation and Child Development Outcomes," in Fatherhood and Family Policy, edited by M.E. Lamb and A. Sagi, Hillside, N.J.: Lawrence Erlbaum, pp. 191–218.

Boys with actively involved fathers tend to get better grades and perform better on achievement tests.

Biller, H.B. 1993, Fathers and Families: Paternal Factors in Child Development, Westport, CT: Auburn House.

Research shows that even very young children who have experienced high father involvement show an increase in curiosity and in problem solving capacity. Fathers' involvement seems to encourage children's exploration of the world around them and confidence in their ability to solve problems.

Pruett, Kyle D. 2000. Fatherneed: Why Father Care is as Essential as Mother Care for Your Child. New York: Free Press.

Highly involved fathers also contribute to increased mental dexterity in children, increased empathy, less stereotyped sex role beliefs and greater self-control.

Abramovitch, H. 1997. Images of the "Father" in The Role of the Father in Child Development. M.E. Lamb, Ed., New York: John Wiley & Sons.

When non-custodial fathers are highly involved with their children's learning, the children are more likely to get A's at all grade levels.

National Center for Education Statistics. October 1997. Fathers' Involvement in Their Children's Schools; National Household Education Survey. NCES 98-091R2. Washington, D.C.: U.S. Department of Education.

Nonresident father contact with children and involvement in their schools within the past year are associated with the same three factors: fathers paying child support; custodial mothers being more educated; and custodial homes not experiencing financial difficulties.

National Center for Education Statistics. October 1997. Fathers' Involvement in Their Children's Schools; National Household Education Survey. NCES 98-091R2. Washington, D.C.: U.S. Department of Education.

High involvement at the early childhood level - frequency with which parents interact with their young children, such as how often they read, tell stories and sign and play with their children. These experiences contribute to children's language and literacy development and transmit information and knowledge about people, places and things.

Bredekamp, S. and Copple, C. 1997. Developmentally Appropriate Practice in Early Childhood Programs. Washington, D.C.: National Association for the Education of Young Children.

A Young Man's Journey Towards A Positive Self-image

According to the National Fatherhood Initiative and the U.S. Census Bureau, out of 24 million children in America — one out of every three — live in biological father-absent homes. Many of the social issues facing America today can be traced back to children growing up without a father. Just look at these astonishing statistics:

- Fatherless children are 100–200% more likely to have emotional and behavioral problems.
- A child who comes from a fatherless home is 68% more likely to use drugs or alcohol, more likely to become sexually active at an early age, and three times more likely to commit a violent crime.
- 63% of teenagers who attempt suicide live in fatherless homes.
- 71% of high school dropouts are from fatherless homes.
- 90% of all homeless and runaway children are from fatherless homes.
- 85% of all youths sitting in prisons grew up in a fatherless home.
- Fatherless sons are 300% more likely to become incarcerated in state juvenile institutions.
- Fatherless daughters who marry have a 92% higher divorce rate, and fatherless sons are 35% more likely to experience marital failure.

- Fatherless daughters are 53% more likely to marry as teenagers, are 111% more likely to have children as teenagers, and are 164% more likely to have an out-of-wedlock birth.
- 80% of teenagers admitted to psychiatric hospitals come from fatherless homes.
- Girls without fathers in their lives are 2 & 1/2 times more likely to get pregnant and 53% more likely to commit suicide.

1. 23.6% of US children (17.4 million) lived in father absent homes in 2014.

[US Census Bureau, 2015] Living arrangements of children under 18 years and marital status of parents, by age, sex, race, and Hispanic origin and selected characteristics of the child for all children: 2014. Washington, D.C.: U.S. Census Bureau.

2. In 2011, children living in female-headed homes with no spouse present had a poverty rate of 47.6%. This is over four times the rate for children living in married couple families.

[Source: U.S. Department of Health & Human Services (2012). Information on poverty and income statistics: A summary of 2012 current population survey data. Retrieved

A Young Man's Journey Towards A Positive Self-image

from: http://aspe.hhs.gov/hsp/12/PovertyAndIncomeEst/ib.cfm]

3. A study of 1,397,801 infants in Florida evaluated how a lack of father involvement impacts infant mortality. A lack of father involvement was linked to earlier births as well as lower birth weights. Researchers also found that father absence increases the risk of infant <u>mortality, and that the mortality rate for infants within the first 28 days of life is four times higher for those with absent fathers than those with involved fathers. Paternal absence is also found to increase black/white infant mortality almost four-fold.</u>

[Source: Alio, A. P., Mbah, A. K., Kornosky, J. L., Wathington, D., Marty, P. J., & Salihu, H. M. (2011). Assessing the impact of paternal involvement on Racial/Ethnic disparities in infant mortality rates. Journal of Community Health, 36(1), 63-68.]

4. A study of 263 13- to 18-year-old adolescent women seeking psychological services found that the adolescents from father-absent homes were 3.5 times more likely to experience pregnancy than

were adolescents from father-present homes. Moreover, the rate of pregnancy among adolescents from father absent homes was 17.4% compared to a four (4) percent rate in the general adolescent population.

[Source: Lang, D. L., Rieckmann, T., DiClemente, R. J., Crosby, R. A., Brown, L. K., & Donenberg, G. R. (2013). Multi-level factors associated with pregnancy among urban adolescent women seeking psychological services. Journal of Urban Health, 90, 212-223.]

5. A study of 1,618 Latina high school students found that lower perceived father support is a predictor of suicidal ideation and behavior.

[Source: De Luca, S. M., Wyman, P., & Warren, K. (2012). Latina adolescent suicide ideations and attempts: Associations with connectedness to parents, peers, and teachers. Suicide and Life-Threat Behavior, 42, 672-683.]

6. Disengaged and remote interactions of fathers with infants is a predictor of early behavior problems in children and can lead to externalizing behaviors in children as early as age 1.

[Source: Ramchandani, P. G., Domoney, J., Sethna, V., Psychogiou, L., Vlachos, H. and Murray, L. (2013). Do early father–infant interactions predict the onset of externalizing behaviors in young children? Findings from a longitudinal cohort study. Journal of Child Psychology and Psychiatry, 54, 56–64.]

7. Researchers using secondary data from the Interuniversity Consortium for Political and Social Research examined gun carrying and drug trafficking in young men, linking father absence to the likelihood of engaging in these behaviors. Results from a sample of 835 juvenile male inmates found that father absence was the only disadvantage on the individual level with significant effects on gun carrying, drug trafficking, and co-occurring behavior. Individuals from father absent homes were found to <u>be 279% more</u> likely to carry guns and deal drugs than peers living with their fathers.

[Source: Allen, A. N., & Lo, C. C. (2012). Drugs, guns, and disadvantaged youths: Co-occurring behavior and the code of the street. Crime & Delinquency, 58(6), 932-953.]

8. A study of the relationship between father absence and lower educational attainment for African American females found that a longer duration of father absence is a predictive factor for lower educational success. Researchers discovered that longer duration of father absence often leads to lower income and family economic stress, which puts young women at risk for lower educational achievement.

[Source: Gillette, M. T., & Gudmunson, C. G. (2014). Processes linking father absence to educational attainment among African American females. Journal of Research on Adolescence, 24(2), 309-321.]

9. Children with negative attitudes about school and their teachers experienced avoidance and ambivalence with their fathers. On the other hand, children with a secure attachment to their father and whose father was involved had a higher academic self-concept. The father-child attachment was more associated with the child's social-emotional school outcomes than their academic achievement.

[Source: Newland, L., Chen, H., & Coyl-Shepherd, D. (2013). Associations among father beliefs, perceptions, life

context, involvement, child attachment and school outcomes in the U.S. and Taiwan. Fathering, 11, 3-30.]

10. Father involvement is related to positive cognitive, developmental, and socio-behavioral child outcomes, such as improved weight gain in preterm infants, improved breastfeeding rates, higher receptive language skills, and higher academic achievement.

[Source: Garfield, C. F., & Isacco, A. (2006). Fathers and the well-child visit, Pediatrics, 117, 637-645.]

11. According to the Bureau of Justice Statistics, the number of children with an incarcerated father grew 79% between 1991 and 2007. Black fathers accounted for nearly half (46%) of all children with an incarcerated father.

[Source: Glaze, L.E., & Maruschak, L.M. (2010). Parents in prison and their minor children. Washington, D.C.: Bureau of Justice Statistics.]

12. Fifty-five (55.2) percent of WIC recipients are raised by single-mothers, 48.2% of all Head

Start recipients are from father-absent homes, and 37% of public assistance and Section 8 housing are female-headed households.

[Source: Nock, S.L, Einolf, C.J. (2008). The one hundred-billion-dollar man: the annual public costs of father absence. Germantown, MD: National Fatherhood Initiative.]

As supported by the data below, children from fatherless homes are more likely to be poor, become involved in drug and alcohol abuse, drop out of school, and suffer from health and emotional problems. Boys are more likely to become involved in crime, and girls are more likely to become pregnant as teens.

1. Poverty

– Children in father-absent homes are almost four times more likely to be poor. In 2011, 12 percent of children in married-couple families were living in poverty, compared to 44 percent of children in mother-only families.

Source: U.S. Census Bureau, Children's Living Arrangements and Characteristics: March 2011, Table C8. Washington D.C.: 2011.

– Children living in female headed families with no spouse present had a poverty rate of 47.6 percent, over 4 times the rate in married-couple families.

Source: U.S. Department of Health and Human Services; ASEP Issue Brief: Information on Poverty and Income Statistics. September 12, 2012 <http://aspe.hhs.gov/hsp/12/PovertyAndIncomeEst/ib.shtml>

Where Is My Father?

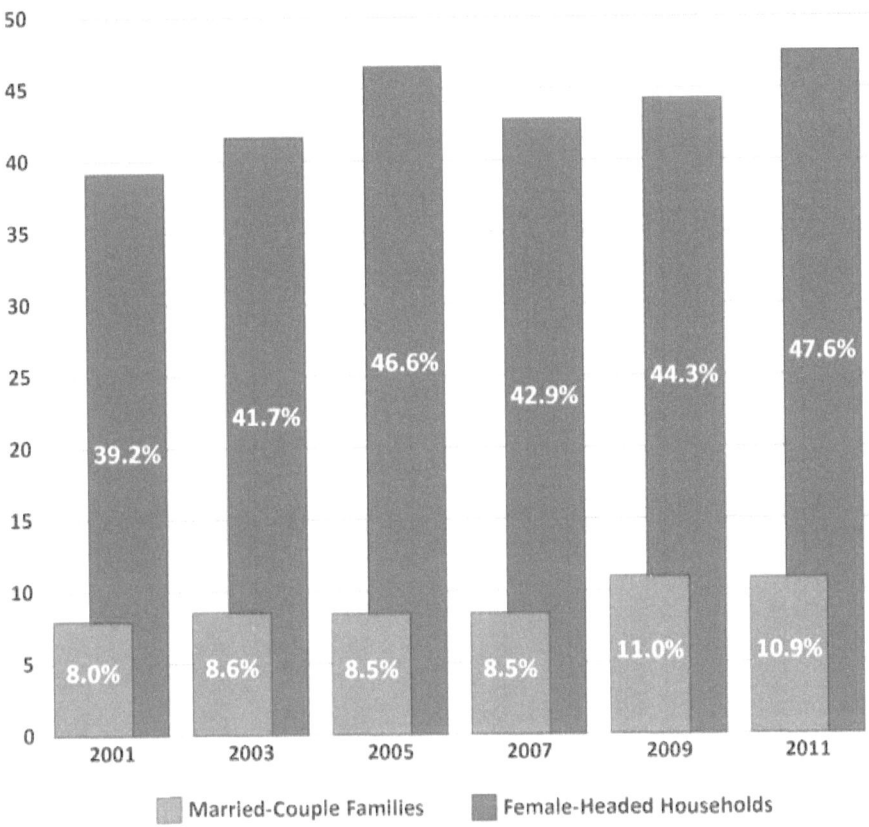

Children in Poverty by Family Structure

Source: U.S. Department of Health and Human Services; ASEP Issue Brief: Information on Poverty and Income Statistics. September 12, 2012 http://aspe.hhs.gov/hsp/12/PovertyAndIncomeEst/ib.shtml

2. Drug and Alcohol Abuse

– The U.S. Department of Health and Human Services states, "Fatherless children are at a dramatically greater risk of drug and alcohol abuse."

Source: U.S. Department of Health and Human Services. National Center for Health Statistics. Survey on Child Health. Washington, DC, 1993.

— There is significantly more drug use among children who do not live with their mother and father.

Source: Hoffmann, John P. "The Community Context of Family Structure and Adolescent Drug Use." Journal of Marriage and Family 64 (May 2002): 314-330.

3. Physical and Emotional Health

— A study of 1,977 children age 3 and older living with a residential father or father figure found that children living with married biological parents had significantly fewer externalizing and internalizing behavioral problems than children living with at least one non-biological parent.

Source: Hofferth, S. L. (2006). Residential father family type and child well-being: investment versus selection. Demography, 43, 53-78.

– Children of single-parent homes are more than twice as likely to commit suicide.

Sources: The Lancet, Jan. 25, 2003 • Gunilla Ringbäck Weitoft, MD, Centre for Epidemiology, the National Board of Health and Welfare, Stockholm, Sweden • Irwin Sandler, PhD, professor of psychology and director of the Prevention Research Center, Arizona State University, Tempe • Douglas G. Jacobs, MD, associate clinical professor of psychiatry, Harvard Medical School; and founder and director, The National Depression Screening Program • Madelyn Gould, PhD, MPH, professor of child psychiatry and public health, College of Physicians and Surgeons, Columbia University; and research scientist, New York State Psychiatric Institute.
<u>http://www.webmd.com/baby/news/20030123/absent-parent-doubles-child-suicide-risk</u>

– Data from three waves of the Fragile Families Study (N= 2,111) was used to examine the prevalence and effects of mothers' relationship changes between birth and age 3 on their children's wellbeing. Children born to single mothers show higher levels of aggressive behavior than children born to married mothers. Living in a single-mother household is equivalent to experiencing 5.25 partnership transitions.

Source: Osborne, C., & McLanahan, S. (2007). Partnership instability and child well-being. Journal of Marriage and Family, 69, 1065-1083.

4. Educational Achievement

– Children in grades 7-12 who have lived with at least one biological parent, youth that experienced divorce, separation, or nonunion birth reported lower grade point averages than those who have always lived with both biological parents.

– Children living with their married biological father tested at a significantly higher level than those living with a nonbiological father.

Source: Tillman, K. H. (2007). Family structure pathways and academic disadvantage among adolescents in stepfamilies. Journal of Marriage and Family.

– Father involvement in schools is associated with the higher likelihood of a student getting mostly A's. This was true for fathers in biological parent families, for stepfathers, and for fathers heading single-parent families.

Source: Nord, Christine Winquist, and Jerry West. Fathers' and Mothers' Involvement in Their Children's Schools by Family Type and Resident Status. (NCES 2001-032). Washington, D.C.: U.S. Department of Education, National Center for Education Statistics, 2001.

– 71% of high school dropouts are fatherless; fatherless children have more trouble academically, scoring poorly on tests of reading, mathematics, and thinking skills; children from father-absent homes are more likely to be truant from school, more likely to be excluded from school, more likely to leave school at age 16, and less likely to attain academic and professional qualifications in adulthood.

Source: Edward Kruk, Ph.D., "The Vital Importance of Paternal Presence in Children's Lives." May 23, 2012. http://www.psychologytoday.com/blog/co-parenting-after-divorce/201205/father-absence-father-deficit-father-hunger

5. Crime

– Adolescents living in intact families are less likely to engage in delinquency than their peers living in non-intact families. Compared to peers in intact families, adolescents in single-parent families and stepfamilies were more likely to engage in delinquency. This relationship appeared to be operating through differences in family processes—parental involvement, supervision, monitoring, and parent-child closeness—between intact and non-intact families.

Source: Stephen Demuth and Susan L. Brown, "Family Structure, Family Processes, and Adolescent Delinquency: The Significance of Parental Absence Versus Parental Gender," Journal of Research in Crime and Delinquency 41, No. 1 (February 2004): 58-81. <u>http://familyfacts.org/briefs/26/marriage-and-family-as-deterrents-from-delinquency-violence-and-crime</u>

— A study using data from the National Longitudinal Study of Adolescent Health explored the relationship between family structure and risk of violent acts in neighborhoods. The results revealed that if the number of fathers is low in a neighborhood, then there is an increase in acts of teen violence. The statistical data showed that a 1% increase in the proportion of single-parent families in a neighborhood is associated with a 3% increase in an adolescent's level of violence.

In other words, adolescents who live in neighborhoods with lower proportions of single-parent families and who report higher levels of family integration commit less violence.

Source: Knoester, C., & Hayne, D.A. (2005). "Community context, social integration into family, and youth violence." Journal of Marriage and Family 67, 767-780.

– Children age 10 to 17 living with two biological or adoptive parents were significantly less likely to experience sexual assault, child maltreatment, other types of major violence, and non-victimization type of adversity, and were less likely to witness violence in their families compared to peers living in single-parent families and stepfamilies.

Source: Heather A. Turner, "The Effect of Lifetime Victimization on the Mental Health of Children and Adolescents," Social Science & Medicine, Vol. 62, No. 1, (January 2006), pp. 13-27.

-A study of 109 juvenile offenders indicated that family structure significantly predicts delinquency.

Source: Bush, Connee, Ronald L. Mullis, and Ann K. Mullis. "Differences in Empathy Between Offender and Non-offender Youth." Journal of Youth and Adolescence 29 (August 2000): 467-478.

6. Sexual Activity and Teen Pregnancy

— A study using a sample of 1409 rural southern adolescents (851 females and 558 males) aged 11 – 18 years, investigated the correlation between father absence and self-reported sexual activity. The results revealed that adolescents in father-absence homes were more likely to report being sexually active compared to adolescents living with their fathers.

Source: Hendricks, C.S., Cesario, S.K., Murdaugh, C., Gibbons, M.E., Servonsky, E.J., Bobadilla, R.V., Hendricks, D.L., Spencer-Morgan, B., & Tavakoli, A. (2005).

– Being raised by a single mother raises the risk of teen pregnancy, marrying with less than a high school degree, and forming a marriage where both partners have less than a high school degree.

Source: Teachman, Jay D. "The Childhood Living Arrangements of Children and the Characteristics of Their Marriages." Journal of Family Issues 25 (January 2004): 86-111.

Where Is My Father?

www.ingramcontent.com/pod-product-compliance
Lightning Source LLC
Chambersburg PA
CBHW021121300426
44113CB00006B/238